The Penn State Series in German Literature

The German Historical Novel in Exile after 1933

The German Historical Novel in Exile after 1933
Calliope Contra Clio

Bruce M. Broerman

The Pennsylvania State University Press
University Park and London

Library of Congress Cataloging-in-Publication Data

Broerman, Bruce M., 1945–
  The German historical novel in exile after 1933.

  (The Penn State series in German literature)
  Includes bibliography and index.
  1. German fiction—20th century—History and criticism.
  2. Historical fiction, German—History and criticism.
  3. German fiction—Foreign countries—History and criticism.
  I. Title. II. Series.
  PT772.B74   1986   833′.081′.09   85-21712
  ISBN 0-271-00421-5

Contents

Preface

Historical fiction was a part of human civilization and culture long before the conception of the written word. It has accompanied man through every phase of his development, and continues as a literary force today. The existence of such a phenomenon, from the epic tales of the ancients to our own modern historical novel, demonstrates an inherent need in man to come to terms with his heritage in literary form. This inherent need, though intangible and indefinable, may have remained basically unchanged, but the expression to which it gives rise in historical fiction has changed repeatedly, sometimes drastically.

It is therefore impossible to subsume the length and breadth of historical fiction under a single definition, for each new era and every new generation interprets its own relationship to its cultural and historical heritage, giving rise to new or modified expression in historical fiction. This in turn forces each new generation of writers and scholars to review and reinterpret historical fiction in its immediate context.

The German historical novel by authors exiled after 1933 is by no means unique. Although 1933 marks the largest migration of scholars and artists into exile known to modern history, it does not obliterate the literary traditions from which the exiled writers came. This study is limited to a representative selection of works by those authors, and the conclusions that are drawn should not be applied directly to other contemporary historical fiction or to historical fiction of past ages. This does not imply, however, that new insights into either or both may not obtain.

The subtitle, *Calliope Contra Clio*, focuses on one of the most basic questions and controversies surrounding the German historical novel of the exile period, and—by extension—the historical novel as a genre *per se*. At the time of Homer no differentiation existed among cognitive modes, and thus none among the muses. With Hesiod's designation of nine muses shortly thereafter in his *Theogony*, however, Calliope became most closely associated with epic poetry while Clio became the benefactress of history with close ties to epic poetry. It could be argued that Clio should have found her legitimate province among the muses no later than Thucydides' *History of the Peloponnesian War*, but this is not the case, for every succeeding generation of writers and critics of historical fiction has had to contend with the question: Is historical fiction indebted primarily to Clio or to Calliope or equally to both?

For the purpose of this study, the initial definition of the historical novel is merely a novel which utilizes history as its material, history which is consciously perceived as belonging to the past, rather than immediate history which finds fictionalized expression in "faction."

A major goal of this study is to raise some of the questions which must be asked before a more comprehensive literary analysis of the German historical novel of the exile period can be undertaken. Since the novels treated range from virtually unknown works to those now part of world literature, no attempt is made at methodological uniformity in the individual analyses. Each analysis in this introductory study takes into account the quality and quantity of existing research. The approach to a little known work or a work which has suffered a long tradition of biased interpretation will necessarily differ from the approach to a work which has undergone comprehensive prior evaluation. In all cases, the analyses are intended not as exhaustive individual studies. Rather this study is intended to be a representative cross-section of works viewed in a greater genre context. In addition, these individual analyses and the conclusions drawn from them should provide a clearer under-standing of the relationship of Calliope and Clio to the German historical novel in exile after 1933.

The text of this study was produced exclusively in English to provide greater access to a neglected area of scholarship. Quotations from both primary and secondary works are taken from definitive English translations, as far as they are available. Where these are lacking, the translations are my own. First references to primary works are fully documented in the Notes; subsequent references are documented in the text by page numbers in parentheses.

Partial support for this project was provided by the Graduate College Research Board of the University of Illinois at Chicago. I owe a special debt of gratitude to my friend, Peter, without whose unflagging encouragement this study could not have been completed.

1
Introduction

Literary genres and modes do not develop in a vacuum, conditioned as they are by the total literary, cultural, and historical tradition and environment. Although the modern historical novel in general traces its beginnings to Sir Walter Scott and late Romanticism and early Realism of the nineteenth century, the literary, cultural, and historical movements developed nationally and individually into the beginning of the twentieth century along such divergent lines that it would be presumptuous to assume a direct line of influence from the historical novels of Scott to the historical novels of German authors exiled after 1933.

In the age of Scott, the course of history itself provided the necessary foundation for the modern historical novel. The French Revolution and the following decades of continental turmoil involved the masses of humanity for the first time in far-reaching political and historical processes. The inevitable result was a new attitude, conscious or unconscious, towards history. History is no longer seen or experienced as a static backdrop against which great figures rise and fall, but as a dynamic process that involves and is shaped by the destinies of the common people.

This new feeling of history and Scott's own endeavors in his translations of Herder's *Volkslieder* and Goethe's *Götz von*

Berlichingen influenced Scott's transition to the historical novel, marked by the appearance of *Waverley* in 1814. Scott's novels are characterized, aside from all shortcomings,[1] by his ability to portray genuine characters in a real historical setting, to re-create an entire epoch which imparts real life, to describe details richly and convincingly, and by his concentration on the common man, who with all his strengths and weaknesses becomes the embodiment of the historical events portrayed.

Historical novels in German literary history took very different approaches, being influenced in varying degrees by the new concept of history and the tradition of Scott. Since they too arose from their total literary, cultural, and historical tradition, they exhibit more dissimilarities than similarities. The highly subjective, idealized, and symbolic world of a past era in Novalis' *Heinrich von Ofterdingen*, for example, contrasts sharply with the glorification of the national past and the genealogy of a family from the time of the tribal migrations to the year 1848 in Gustav Freytag's *Die Ahnen*.

The historical distance between these two works can explain much of the dissimilarity. The contrast of contemporaries is just as great, however, if one compares, for instance, C. F. Meyer's *Jürg Jenatsch,* in which historical material is used to achieve distance and objectivity for the psychological portrayal of individuals, with Georg Ebers' *Eine ägyptische Königstochter,* which dwells on the learned archeological-antiquarian aspect of history for its own sake. Equally dissimilar would be the psychological portraits of society in the historical novels of Theodor Fontane and the biographical novels of Stefan Zweig.

This problem is understandable, since the term "historical novel" refers traditionally only to content. This traditional concept is still prevalent today, especially among those who fail to differentiate between the historical novels of one age and those of another, or who try to equate, in some manner, the historical novel with historiography, Calliope with Clio.

The contention that the historical novel is a re-creation of history for its own sake, a form of history, and a legitimate approach to history may be true, to a limited extent, for certain ages and certain authors, but it fails when applied to the entire genre.[2] Equally false is the contention that the historical novel is determined by artificial restrictions on the subject matter, dependent on whether the author writes from personal or externally acquired experience.[3] These views, along with the contention that all writing is historical and therefore all novels are historical novels,[4] constitute usages of the term which are either so limited or so broad as to render them useless to literary scholars investigating the historical novel of a specific age.

All novels do have historical value and significance in varying degrees. The conscious selection of material from an age past for a fictional work, however, immediately distinguishes that work from those which utilize contemporary material or material from the realm of fantasy. It is therefore entirely proper to speak of the historical novel as a distinct genre. But the treatment of the historical novel over the years as a bastard genre, mothered mainly by Clio, is responsible for much of the confusion attending the concept today.

This confusion has also been a major obstacle for literary scholars in coming to terms with the German historical novel in exile. However, the historical novel has never been a static entity, but is in itself a historical phenomenon which has evolved through centuries of literary history with each writer interpreting its role, significance, and function to suit his own purposes. When the modern literary scholar speaks of the historical novel, moreover, the primary interest should be in the "novel" aspect as a literary art form and never in the "historical" aspect as a form of history. Most attempts in the past to combine history and creative fiction in novel form have succeeded at neither. This, of course, does not preclude the necessity on the part of the literary scholar to concern himself with the particular historical period being portrayed.

It is true that the historical novelist can render personages, events, and entire periods of history more vividly than the historian. It is equally true that the historical novelist can, in some cases, give a historically accurate portrayal of a past era. When these become major ends in themselves, however, we are no longer dealing with the creative literary artist, but more with the writer of popular romance.

The dual nature of the historical novel—the influence of both Calliope and Clio—and the diversity possible within the genre are taken into account by those who offer significant approaches to the German historical novel.[5] Max Wehrli, for example, postulates a typology based on the literary intent or plot.[6] He distinguishes three main types: historical belles lettres, which requires strict adherence to historical facts and thus tries to compete with historiography; the cultural-historical novel, which attempts to portray the symbolic truth of historical material directed towards a particular cultural community and requires factualness only as far as it serves the created myth; and the ethical-religious historical novel, historical fiction in the form of a theodocy, which maintains little more than a historical format. These three categories clearly represent the extent to which the literary work is bound to historical material, revealing a trend from historical objectivity to historical subjectivity.

Equally significant is the view of Bernhard Rang, who sees the task of the genuine historian as well as the creative novelist expressed in the recognition and portrayal of history as a progressive, living force.[7] Where the historian deals with facts in order to interpret them in relationship to one another, however, the historical novelist deals with facts for their inner symbolic meaning. Thus, the historical novelist gives new meaning to history, portrays it symbolically, elevates it to myth. The creative writer utilizes history as a perspective, distant from the chaos of the present, in order to intensify his portrayal of intellectual and spiritual experiences and to sublimate the portrayal of man and humanity. History remains incidental, offering only a framework and background. Only by transcending the purely historical, through subjective transformation, does the historical novel shed the problematical stigma of a hybrid literary form.

Georg Lukács' theory of the historical novel is decidedly biased and of limited application to the German historical novel of the exile period, conditioned as it is by his political orientation and the age in which it was written.[8] In his materialistic treatment of literary history, he sees the task of the historical novelist as portraying the interaction of socio-economic developments and artistic form as it affects the historical consciousness of the masses and of leading historical personalities. In tracing the transformation of the historical novel from Sir Walter Scott to the late 1930s, he examines the influence of such contradictory views as those of Ranke and Nietzsche on the concept of history and thus on the historical novel.[9] In this transformation, he sees a continual decline of his concept of realism in the historical novel, a decline which reaches its nadir in the fascist falsifications and mythicization of history. Since it equates political and economic facts of life with artistic expression in literature, Lukács' theory is very limited and can only be read within the framework of "Socialist Realism," and that only so far as it reflects his view of "Socialist Realism."[10]

Lion Feuchtwanger, one of the most prolific writers of historical novels among the German exiles, offers a general theory of the historical novel that centers on his perception of the relationship between historiography and imaginative historical writing. Historiography provides the mere skeleton of historical fact, whereas it is the imagination of the poet that provides the living flesh of historical truth which may have little connection to historical fact.[11] An author may select historical material for any number of reasons, but the content always remains contemporary and under the author's subjective control. This view follows from the contention that, while the creative writer can only express his relationship to his own time and his own personal experience, an author can portray a contemporary view of the world only if he distances himself from it. Historical material provides a ready-made perspective for such a distance.

Both Lukács and Feuchtwanger emphasize the necessity for the historical novel to provide a connection between the past and the present, but they see radically different purposes. Feuchtwanger points out the weaknesses of Lukács' theory, stressing that although great historical movements can, though they do not always, motivate a poet to create great historical works, great historical literature can also come into being quite apart from any such stimuli. Opposed to the restricted view of Lukács' Marxist aesthetics, Feuchtwanger acknowledges the artistic freedom of the writer. Where Lukács makes the novels of Scott an archetype, against which all successive historical novels are to be measured, Feuchtwanger views Scott only as the founder of the tradition of the serious modern historical novel.

Alfred Döblin, another exiled German author of historical novels, developed a theory of the historical novel that in many respects approaches that of Feuchtwanger. He initially viewed the historical novel as the last vestige of the ancient oral tradition of the epics, whose function it was to collect, preserve, and transmit the reality, not the mere facts, of great historical events and personages.[12] According to Döblin, a creative writer selects historical material because it activates his "sensitive artistic resonator," allowing him to create a fictitious reality. Not until this fictitious historical reality merges with the reality of the author's own experience does a true historical novel emerge.

Under the phenomenon of exile, Döblin modifies this view to recognize the viability of the historical novel as an expression of the immediate contemporary world.[13] He rejects unconditionally all attacks on the historical novel as cowardly escapes from reality or as anachronistic literary art forms. He sees the proliferation of the historical novel in exile as well as within the Third Reich as a result of the historical situation of the authors. In both cases, the authors attempt to come to terms with the threatening situation inside Germany by seeking historical parallels for that which they experience but are unable to express directly: for those inside the Third Reich because it is forbidden, for those in exile because they are removed from the actuality of events. Döblin justifiably discredits those historical novels written within the Third Reich which were nothing more than extensions of Nazi propaganda. Closely related to Döblin's theory is Heinrich Mann's contention that one cannot avoid viewing historical events and personages as applied examples of one's own experience.[14]

Looking back at the history of the German historical novel, one cannot doubt that the widespread preference of a large audience for the professorial novels of Dahn and Ebers led to a decline in the prestige of the historical novel as literary art. In addition, such novels were seen by many to characterize in general the historical novel as a genre, fueling for succeeding generations the controversy as to whether Calliope or Clio should be accorded the position as its legitimate muse. In the first three decades of the twentieth century, however, especially under the influence of Neo-Romanticism,[15] the historical novel experienced a rebirth that proliferated under different guises, attested to by the divergent forms the genre assumed under Ricarda Huch, Jakob Wassermann, Alfred

Döblin, Max Brod, Heinrich Mann, Eduard Stucken, Franz Werfel, Lion Feuchtwanger, Alfred Neumann, and Ina Seidel, to name only a few.[16]

Besides these trends, a new form of the historical novel developed, one which led into the national socialist movement, a trend towards a more powerful, masculine, nationalistic expression. But even here there are differences between, for example, the more serious intentions of Erwin Guido Kolbenheyer's novels and the more entertaining novels or even subliterature of Hans Friedrich Blunck, Mirko Jelusisch, or Robert Hohlbaum.[17]

With the beginning of exile, however, the historical novel acquired a new meaning for different reasons. The causes for the proliferation of this genre, especially in exile, are varied. First, a natural tendency exists for historical treatments of material to arise in an exile situation. The author who is severed from his own world desires to seek historical parallels, to orient and justify oneself historically. The historical novel thus becomes a form of self-preservation.[18]

For economic and psychological reasons, writers in exile could ill afford to engage in avant-garde literary experiments. Cut off from their homeland, they wanted to continue their own literary tradition, in literary content as well as in language, because they saw the usurpers of power in Germany distorting all traditions. Historical novels, especially those that try to come to terms with the immediate present, offered a framework for the preservation and continuation of the "genuine" German literary tradition as they saw it.[19]

The tendency toward parody among the exiled writers led them to favor the historical *roman à clef*, which permitted them to mock the hated usurpers of power in historical costume without naming their adversaries directly, allowing the exiles to avoid immortalizing the names of those they hated.[20] Many authors were also guided by aesthetic and creative instincts to an indirect (i.e., historical) treatment of material that would safeguard their presentation from becoming mere reportage laden with tendentious cliché.[21]

Although the historical novel has become a subject of increasing interest in research devoted to German literature in exile after 1933, a comprehensive view is still lacking. This is undoubtedly due, in part, to the fact that exile literature has only recently found general acceptance as a distinct phenomenon in twentieth-century literature, and the wealth of materials is still in various stages of discovery and collection. Another factor contributing to this lack is the sheer number of historical novels written by exiled German authors. The availability of these hundreds of novels, many of which have remained in or fallen into obscurity, is still limited in some cases.

As can be expected, literary histories of modern German literature have little to offer. In some cases, German literature in exile, and thus the historical novel in exile, is ignored. In other cases, exile literature may be treated, but the historical novel receives only incidental or indirect coverage. Those literary histories that do include sections on the historical novel in exile are too general to be significant, betray misconceptions of the historical novel, or reveal, in the case of Marxist critics, a fatally limited view.

The growing secondary literature devoted to German literature in exile after 1933 gives increasing attention to the historical novel. Klaus Jarmatz, for example, discusses the historical novel as it relates to the literary creation of a new picture of man and humanity in *Literatur im Exil*,[22] but only in communist terms. Matthias Wegner's *Exil und Literatur: Deutsche Schriftsteller im Ausland 1933–1945*[23] includes a section devoted to the controversy surrounding the historical novel in exile, an aspect which receives a more thorough treatment in "Literarische Kontroversen innerhalb der Exil-Literatur der dreissiger Jahre"[24] by Dagmar Malone, who also traces the chronology of the controversy. The format and scope of Alexander Stephan's *Die deutsche Exilliteratur 1933–1945*[25] are similar to that of Wegner's work, precluding comprehensive treatment of particular genres. *Exil in den USA mit einem Bericht "Schanghai—Eine Emigration am Rande"*[26] is also very general in nature, devotes little space to literature, and, apart from minimal comments on individual novels, does nothing to illuminate the historical novel as a genre in the exile period. *Exil und innere Emigration*[27] includes an article by Klaus Schröter, "Der historische Roman. Zur Kritik seiner spätbürgerlichen Erscheinung," that traces the development of the historical novel into the thirties and discusses the genre inside and outside of the Third Reich. Due to Schröter's Marxist approach, however, his interpretation of individual novels and of the genre in general is biased and of limited significance. The format of both *Die deutsche Exilliteratur 1933–1945*,[28] edited by Manfred Durzak, and *Deutsche Exilliteratur seit 1933: I: Kalifornien*,[29] edited by John M. Spalek and Joseph P. Strelka, precludes any specific treatment of the historical novel *per se*, but both books do include several articles on major authors of historical novels in exile. As the approach is general, however, individual novels receive very brief discussions, an exception being Durzak's own article on Hermann Broch's *The Death of Virgil*. The title of Günther Heeg's *Die Wendung zur Geschichte: Konstitutionsprobleme antifaschistischer Literatur im Exil*[30] reveals its basic socio-political approach, and his chapter devoted to the historical novel of bourgeois antifascist writers discusses only Feuchtwanger and Heinrich Mann. A similar approach is evident in *Erfahrung Exil: Antifaschistische Romane 1933–1945*,[31] edited by Sigrid Bock and Manfred Hahn, which, however, offers more thorough discussions of individual works. *Das Exilerlebnis*,[32] edited by Donald G. Daviau and Ludwig M. Fischer, includes a section devoted to the historical novel, but here, too, the emphasis is on individual works or a single aspect of several works. Due to a misunderstanding of the nature of the historical novel, Heinz Dieter Osterle excludes such works in "Die Deutschen im Spiegel des sozialkritischen Romans der Emigranten 1933–1950,"[33] for he presupposes that they could not be the literary vehicle of valid social criticism nor have relevance to the twentieth century.

Secondary works devoted exclusively to the German historical novel in exile have thus far approached the subject from very specific viewpoints. In "Untersuchungen zum historischen Roman der deutschen Emigrantenliteratur nach 1933,"[34] Carl Steiner attempts to show that a new appraisal of the historical novel occurred in exile which connected it to the humanistic tradition of German literature and continued the fight against Nazism. Around the central idea that the one factor unifying all exile literature is the concern for the preservation of the values of Western Civilization, an idea which in itself is open to debate, Steiner organizes the discussion of the novels as a progression of Western thought from Biblical times through the nineteenth century. Although he undoubtedly contributes to the scholarship on the German historical novel in exile by analyzing individual works, his discussion is rooted in the most superficial criterion, the historical material itself.

Hans Dahlke's "Geschichtsroman und Literaturkritik im Exil"[35] concentrates mainly on the literary criticism of the historical novels written by exiles as expressed by exiled contemporaries. His discussion, however, is conditioned by his communist views of literature and history and their relationship to one another. Whereas he treats the authors of historical novels in exile as a more or less homogeneous group, which they were not, he sees a schism occurring after the war. Predictably, this schism runs along ideological lines: Dahlke singles out writers of communist sympathies as being most capable of developing and continuing an unbroken literary tradition in the "historically conscious literary community of the East." Though his treatment is useless as objective literary criticism, his bibliography is valuable as a guide to contemporary criticism of the historical novel in exile.

Elke Nyssen, in *Geschichtsbewusstsein und Emigration: Der historische Roman der deutschen Antifaschisten 1933–1945*,[36] treats the historical novels of the exiled writers from the standpoint of historical consciousness and anti-fascist political engagement. The central idea, therefore, is similar to that of Steiner. She draws together many aspects of previous studies in her discussion of the controversy surrounding the historical novel in exile and the historical novel inside and outside of the Third Reich. The individual studies of the novels concentrate on their particular role in the anti-fascist struggle. There is only a very small measure of literary analysis, for the novels are criticized and evaluated solely from this socio-political standpoint. This approach leads her to classify certain novels as escapist literature, an escape from the historical necessity of bearing the anti-fascist banner. Not only does she misinterpret these particular novels, a direct result of her failure to view the novels as a totality of form and content, but she also reduces the historical novel in exile to a mere political tool. From a literary viewpoint, therefore, one would be justified in dismissing the historical novel in exile entirely, for this interpretation reduces it to the level of the fascist historical novels written in the Third Reich, the only difference being their opposing political attitudes.

The most encouraging studies to date are those of Renate Werner and Helmut Koopmann.[37] Werner discusses the German historical novel of the exiles in the context of the traditions out of which it arose, emphasizing the model and analogous character in novels by Stefan Zweig, Lion Feuchtwanger, Heinrich Mann, and Bertolt Brecht. Koopmann expands on this approach both in terms of theory and in comprehensiveness by postulating a tripartite typology (analogy, parallel, parable) as the basis for discussing the aesthetics of the German historical novel of the exile period.

There is little doubt that Walter A. Berendsohn's initial assessment of the novels written in exile—that many are worthless as literature, though valuable as documents of the time—is correct.[38] This view, however, has been repeated and emphasized to such a degree that literary discussions of exile literature in general and the historical novel in particular have been almost non-existent. As a review of secondary literature indicates, there is a wealth of material concerned with the political, social, psychological, philosophical, and thematic aspects of the historical novel in exile. This overemphasizing of secondary aspects, especially the political, is easy enough to understand: The specter of the moral and historical catastrophe embodied by Hitler and the Third Reich is still very much a part of our contemporary thinking. But it is exactly for this reason that a new approach to the historical novel in exile is demanded, for literature, as a literary art form, does not survive on the basis of political engagement or any other limited individual aspect; it can survive only on its merits as literary art.

What is needed, therefore, is an initial study that both investigates the literary viability of the historical novel in exile and takes into account all the various aspects of the individual novels. This requires, first of all, a new or fresh view, or, in some cases, merely a review of a cross-section of the historical novels written by German authors exiled after 1933. A careful analysis of the individual novels will then allow certain tentative conclusions to be drawn which could provide the basis for a more comprehensive study of the genre as a whole as it relates to the exile period. The aim of the following analyses and the conclusions drawn from them is not, therefore, completeness, but rather an initial plotting of the direction literary scholarship must take if the historical novel in exile is to be accorded significance beyond that of a mere footnote in a literary history. Thus, the selection of novels does not depend on ideological, political, sociological, thematic, psychological, or philosophical considerations; it is a representative cross-section of the approaches to historical material writers use to produce literary art, a literary battleground between Calliope and Clio.

2
Analyses

Wolfgang Cordan
Julian the Enlightened One

Wolfgang Cordan, one of the many German writers and intellectuals who fled after Hitler came to power, witnessed firsthand the negative forces of Nazism from his vantage point among the Dutch underground resistance movement.[1] Like so many of the German exiled writers, he turned to the historical novel as a forum for advocating a spiritual rebirth of modern man to counter the evil of the dehumanizing totalitarianism rampant in his age.

For this purpose Cordan chose the figure of Flavius Claudius Julianus—Julian the Apostate, as he became known to history—whom he transforms into a type of Messiah in his novel, *Julian the Enlightened One*.[2] Julian becomes the symbolic embodiment of spiritual rebirth, a messianic figure exhibiting many parallels to the figure of Christ but conceived as the antithesis of Christ, for Cordan consciously employs images of Christianity and the Christian tradition in order to contradict them. Cordan's indebtedness to Clio is clearly revealed in the

breadth of historical fact and wealth of documentation, but
Calliope structures the whole, determines the various themes
and their interrelationships, and thus transforms the novel into
a literary symbol of universal import with indirect but very
definite reference to the contemporary world of Cordan's day.

In the quadripartite structure of the novel, each of the four
books represents a major station in Julian's life, and each is
dominated by a theme that characterizes that particular station.
Book I, for example, is dominated by the search for truth, for
Julian is driven from within to seek ultimate knowledge, the
Light of Truth. The theme of friendship is the characteristic
feature of Book II, in which Julian attracts an expanding circle
of friends and loyal followers. Book III, in which Julian is
charged with establishing political and military order in Gaul,
is dominated by the theme of order. Book IV, which reflects
Julian's transformation to Julianus Illuminatus Invictus, bears
the aspect of final dynamic achievement, portrayed in Julian's
attempts to effect in the world his own inner transformation
and the leadership abilities he gained in Gaul.

These dominant themes reflect the expanding nature of
Julian's self. The emphasis in Book I, for example, is on the
relationship between Julian and his inner self, in Book II on the
relationship between Julian's inner self and an expanding circle of friends, in Book III on the relationship between Julian
and the political sphere of the Western Empire, and in Book IV
on the relationship between Julian and the entire worldly empire and the ultimate reunion of the inner self with Helios-
Mithra.

The character of Julian is inextricably associated with the
two figures who play the key roles in his life: Euhemeros and
Jamblichos.[3] As exemplified in their outer appearances, these
two figures are opposites: Euhemeros is a figure of Darkness,
Jamblichos of Light (29, 212–14). On the other hand, both
figures represent homoerotic Eros-Anteros relationships with
Julian, although in different spheres. Euhemeros rules and represents the physical, worldly realm, the realm rooted in
Julian's birth as an imperial prince, whereas Jamblichos rules
and represents the inner, divine realm, the entire body of Greek
culture and thought, that element within Julian which drives

him to seek and find the Light of Truth. As such, these two figures are clearly symbolic of Julian's duality.

The points at which Euhemeros and Jamblichos enter and leave the novel enhance the symbolic nature of the figures. Euhemeros enters in the third chapter of the first book, the point at which Julian consciously begins to assume the role of an imperial prince, and remains constantly at Julian's side, preceding him in death on the Persian battlefield. Jamblichos does not appear until the beginning of the second book, when Julian has already undergone his inner transformation through the encounters with Libanios and Maximos. As a physical presence, he appears only in the second book; thereafter he appears to Julian only in dreams.

Julian is aware of his double nature, but at first does not perceive it as belonging to two different spheres. That is why his attempt to find the ultimate truth of the mysteries of life and the universe through the snake cult of Euhemeros ends in revulsion and despair. Euhemeros, however, even after being drawn away from the snake cult by Julian, remains Julian's personal snake god and rules his heart. In symbolic terms, Julian's life is bound to the worldly: he cannot and does not wish to reject his role as a prince destined to become emperor. Euhemeros' Dance of the Soul or Snake Dance enhances his dual role as character and symbol of the worldly realm. This dance precedes Julian's marriage to Helena, the symbolic bond between him and the worldly realm of empire. This marriage or bond, however, literally and symbolically has no future. Just as the political insanity of the worldly realm assures that Julian will receive no heir, his attempts in the worldly realm have no direct visible influence on posterity.

There is a clear parallel from the very beginning of the relationship between Julian and Jamblichos to the Zeus-Ganymede relationship (216, 224–31, 241, 424). The symbolic significance of Jamblichos' relationship to Julian, however, is transformed from that of Ganymede to that of Genius, a change which is expressed in Jamblichos' words preceding his suicide: " 'The eagle now flies to the sun, but I am Ganymede no longer' " (424). Jamblichos defines his role as Julian's Genius in the dream Julian experiences after sending the two letters to Constantius, the one acquiescing in the demand to relinquish troops for the Persian campaign, the other an open challenge to Constantius' ability to rule: " 'Since I left my body, I have always been near you, nearer than I ever was in life. That's why I left like Antinoos, so that I could become your Genius. I may reveal myself to you today, I will come once more, when I call you to me. Farewell and complete your mission' " (455). This change in aspect is, of course, the reason that Jamblichos appears as a physical presence only in Book II and thereafter only in Julian's dreams as an invisible influence.

The symbolic figures of Euhemeros and Jamblichos clearly show on the one hand that Julian is destined to and desires to fulfill his role in the worldly chaotic realm. On the other hand, he is driven by his intellect and inner soul to apply the principles of Eros to the world of Chaos and to consummate the ultimate reunion of his individual soul with Helios-Mithra. Since these two figures are concretizations of portions of Julian's own person, the relationships involved, and thus the imagery, can only be homoerotic.

The dichotomy of the Euhemeros-Jamblichos aspects within Julian carries over into the dichotomy of Eros versus Chaos, a theme which pervades the entire work. It is clear that Julian's life becomes an attempt to apply order through the principles of Eros to the worldly realm of Chaos. Before the encounter with Libanios, however, Julian shrinks from the thought of someday being forced to rule over men, for he is struck by the basic depravity of man and the chaotic state of the world. From Libanios he learns the role Eros is to play: " 'the only important thing is insight into the beneficence of the Creator and his intent to nullify the adversity of the elements and to give form to the realm of wildly erratic matter. This is the meaning of the formula: Eros versus Chaos' " (90).

Mardonios, the Scythian eunuch who raised Julian, explains how this principle applies to the political world: " 'All evil in this world derives from the so-called men of action who think they can dispense with the intellect and do everything with their hands. They succeed only in churning up the infinite realm of the material world without ever giving it form. Only spirit can create form. The true ruler must be a combination scholar, priest, consul and, when necessary, soldier' "

(126–27). This is, of course, an exact portrayal of Julian's life and, at the same time, a counterimage of Julian's and Cordan's eras.

As Julian gradually assumes his imperial role, he applies the ordering principles of Eros to his chaotic world. In the first book, Julian is not yet in command of these principles and thus worldly chaos determines the outer course of his life. In Book II, he is in command of these principles, but has as yet no real function within the chaos of the empire. Thus his influence is limited to his immediate circle of friends and followers. In the third book, Julian successfully applies these principles to chaos, but, since the area of his influence is still limited, the chaos of the world dominates and almost destroys him. In Book IV, Julian finally has command over the entire worldly chaos and proceeds to apply the principles of Eros through far-reaching reforms.

These attempts, however, do not lead to a reform of mankind, and in one respect they actually fail completely. But as Julian recognizes at his death: " 'No one completes everything, one can only complete *oneself* " (540). Success or failure at such attempts is therefore irrelevant. The value and ultimate success of such endeavors are inherent in their being attempted. Julian's words concerning Socrates and Christ apply to himself: " 'If the deeds of one's life are to have symbolic meaning, it is not enough *that* one's fate is endured, but rather *how*' " (431). Julian becomes a symbol, and the fulfillment of his destiny, the manner in which he accomplishes it are the basis for the symbolic significance of his life.

Equally important and closely connected to the dichotomy of Eros versus Chaos is the dichotomy of Julian versus Christ. Julian, like Christ, is perceived as a saviour, but in all he represents, he is in fact diametrically opposed to the figure of Christ. This rather complex relationship is suggested in the title itself, for, historically, Julian is known as "the Apostate." While changing this to "the Enlightened One" or "Illuminatus" does not equate him with Christ, it does remove the negative stigma of the historical appellation and raise him to a level of a higher order.

In the novel countless parallels in actions and imagery identify Julian with Christ. Before Julian returns from Ephesos to

Pergamon, he shares a last meal of bread and wine with the members of the Mithras cult (185). Julian's march to the East evokes from an observer the comment: "he looks as mighty as Christ the King on Judgement Day" (471). His tumultuous arrival in Constantinople is an imperial version of Christ's entry into Jerusalem (478–79). The portents surrounding Jesus' death—earthquakes, the rending of the veil in the Temple— find their counterparts in the final stage of Julian's life: earthquakes, the collapse of the Mithras temple, the crumbling of the rebuilt walls of Solomon's Temple (520–21). All of Julian's attempts appear to have been in vain, and his utterance of despair as the signs turn against him—" 'Where have I failed, that the gods should desert me?' " (521)—clearly echoes Christ's " 'My God, my God, why hast thou forsaken me?' " (Matthew 27:46; Mark 15:34). Moreover, Julian's dying utterance, " 'Water' " (540), recalls Christ's " 'I thirst' " (John 19:28).

On the other hand, it is clear that Julian is not a Christ figure in the Christian sense. Throughout the novel, the figure and significance of Christ are juxtaposed to the figure and significance of Socrates, and through him, of Julian. The words of the Athenian philosopher Priskos in reference to Socrates reflect Julian and his beliefs: " 'The earthly life of the Galilean is assuredly one of touching symbolism: a picturebook of all human frailties. Desertion, betrayal, and, in the end, despair of god. Socrates praised god with his last breath and his friends stood by him. His path is more difficult, to be sure, he relieves man of nothing, but shows instead how man can advance step by step toward the Good and the Beautiful through strict discipline and the force of an ever-vigilant will' " (329).

Julian rejects the Christian concept of salvation and all intimations on the part of others that he is a Messiah, even a Messiah of Helios-Mithra: " 'I cannot resurrect him, weak mortal that I am, I can merely reawaken in man a reverence for his immense greatness, in which we all partake. It is for that reason that I have come' " (479). This rejection of a Messiah role reverses the imagery of Christ in the figure of Julian. The Jewish girl, Chaja, dances for Julian, presenting the suffering of her people, and then asks: " 'When will the Messiah come?' " to which Julian answers: " 'Shed no more tears, my daughter. I am not the Messiah. I am the Emperor of the World who will lead your scattered people back to their holy land' " (495–96).[4]

In spite of the parallel to Christ in Julian's request for water at the end of the novel, the imagery is again reversed. The idea of Christ dying on the cross for the redemption of man's sins through the fall of Adam is completely altered. Julian's request for water is associated with the state of existence of the Adamites, a state of innocence before the fall. Since the Adamites live in harmony with God and the world, from which they have withdrawn, they have no need of a Messiah. This underscores the fact that Julian is not a Messiah figure, for in death, despite following an entirely different path that leads directly through the world, he attains the harmony characteristic of the Adamites.

The complexity of the Julian figure as a Christ figure that is at the same time diametrically opposed to Christ is reflected in the structure of the novel. It cannot be coincidence that the novel is divided into four books, each of which has a dominant theme. Nor can it be coincidence that these dominant themes correspond to the four fixed signs of the zodiac in a particular order: Book I—Scorpio, Book II—Aquarius, Book III—Taurus, and Book IV—Leo. Recalling the teaching of Eugenios in astral symbolism (169) and the Biblical references that connect the four Gospels to the same fixed signs (Ezek. 1:10 and Rev. 4:7), the significance of this structure becomes clear. The order of the Gospels indicated in Revelation (i.e., Mark, Luke, Matthew, John) represents the astrological correspondences of Leo, Taurus, Aquarius, and Scorpio: in other words, a progression in order exactly opposite to the books of the novel.

Through the figure of Julian, Cordan has created a symbol with which he poses a basic question to his contemporary world: Does or can the Hellenistic spirit, the heritage of Antiquity, the spirit of Eros, survive today?[5] Cordan is convinced that the misfortunes of modern man, no less than those of men of the past, result from a failure to grasp the Hellenistic spirit as embodied in Julian.[6] He views this spirit as a part of man which may be periodically suppressed, but which always emerges anew. Cordan's own age was one of suppression—in astrological terms, the Age of Pisces. Cordan, however, sees modern man on the threshold of a new age, symbolized in the dawning of the Age of Aquarius, and poses to his contemporaries the question: What does the Water Carrier signify for modern man?[7] He does not answer the question directly, for the answer lies in man's perception of that which Julian represents.

Cordan is actually calling for a spiritual rebirth of man, a rebirth not connected to the orthodoxy of any religion, but to the principle of Eros as embodied in Julian. This is the basis for the symbol of Julian as a Christ figure diametrically opposed to Christ. In Cordan's view, Christianity, by accommodating itself to the chaos of the world, assured both its widespread external survival and its inefficacy and impotence for preserving the principles of Eros. This is the reason Julian cautions Cumonis and Eugenios against giving Mithraism a firm dogma.

By looking back, by presenting the transformed historical figure of Julian, Cordan is pointing forward. Through the words of Julian, which characterize his own path to enlightenment, Cordan speaks to his contemporary world: " 'The path from Plato to Plotinus is laid out in the books and there is no need of salvation. Enlightenment, the opening up of the heavens, the incarnate experience of perfection is a gift of the Allmighty which is granted those who genuinely strive for its attainment' " (431–32). The goal of man, then, is not salvation in the Christian sense, but enlightenment, insight into the totality of existence which combines the rational and irrational, the finite and the infinite, Euhemeros and Jamblichos. This insight is gained by studying and perceiving the symbolic significance of great figures of the past and applying this insight to one's own life. Cordan does not stop with personal enlightenment, however, for enlightenment is only the prerequisite for human action in the finite sphere of worldly chaos.

The novel proclaims that, in spite of the prevailing influence of Chaos in the world, the Hellenistic spirit and the principles of Eros are not lost.[8] The sphere of influence for these principles is extremely limited, but they are passed on from generation to generation, often so endangered that they can survive only secretly, especially in times of great suppression. This idea, of course, is connected to Cordan's own activities during Hitler's years in power: Adherents of the Hellenistic spirit, both inside and outside of Germany, had to work secretly to accomplish whatever goals the chaos of the times would allow.

What Cordan may wish to imply by pitting Christianity against Mithraism in his portrayal of Julian is that only an extreme eclecticism—characteristic of the historical Julian's brand of Mithraism—can genuinely fill the existential vacuum for modern man. In the hands of Cordan, the figure of Julian thus becomes a counterfigure to the dictators of the twentieth century. As a totality, *Julian the Enlightened One* becomes a symbol for the principles of Eros and the Hellenistic spirit and an example of how this spirit can be preserved and transmitted to coming generations.

Bruno Frank
A Man Called Cervantes

When Bruno Frank's *Cervantes*[9] was first published, it was variously referred to as a biography, a biography which was both history and poetry, a novelized biography, a fictionalized biography, and a biographical novel.[10] In all of these cases, the emphasis was on the word "biography"; thus the real significance of this historical novel was overlooked. This may have been a contributing factor for adding the subtitle *A Novel* in the 1944 edition.[11]

It cannot be denied, of course, that the life of Miguel de Cervantes Saavedra is the subject matter of the novel, nor can it be denied that Frank adheres in most cases to the meager historically documented information on Cervantes' life.[12] This is only the historical material of the novel, however, and does not reflect the intent or the significance of the novel as literary art. Frank chose this historical material not primarily because he was interested in Cervantes' life per se, but because he saw in the life and age of Cervantes historical material which could mirror his own development as a writer and the age in which he lived.

Ernst Toller sees Frank's purpose when he discusses the relationship between the novel and the era: "In the confusion of the times people seek a meaning in the ideas and life of others, hope for some gain in practical wisdom, but learn in the end that experience is not to be purchased, that it must be lived."[13] Toller points out that the lessons of the past cannot be applied directly to one's own age or life, "but nevertheless the copybooks of others have a significance: for they may give us strength to endure our own roads, our own despairs, struggles, fate."[14]

Frank's Cervantes is thus a representative figure, for he exemplifies the fate of Frank and many of his contemporaries. Frank's own life and personality reveal the kindred spirit he perceived in the person of Cervantes and in the figure of Don Quixote, so that a definite parallel—Cervantes-Don Quixote-Bruno Frank—emerges.[15] Frank creates a Cervantes who himself becomes the Don Quixote he created, the scorned but wise madman pursuing and seeking to preserve the good and just in an evil, morally corrupt, and unjust world, a world in which reality and that which passes for reality stand in stark contrast. What Cervantes accomplished in writing *Don Quixote*, Frank, as a representative for many of his contemporaries who fled the evils, injustices, and moral corruption of Hitler's Germany, accomplishes in writing *Cervantes*.

Frank and many of his exiled contemporaries were, in effect, companions in fate of Cervantes' Don Quixote and Frank's Cervantes. The vast majority of them witnessed the destruction and disillusionment of World War I, experienced the economic disaster, the moral decay and disillusionment of the Twenties, and watched with horror as Nazism arose and spread throughout Germany. This was their school of life, not unlike that of Frank's Cervantes. Those who had a sense of justice, humanity, and morality were ignored, scorned, and finally driven into exile. The only weapon left to them was the pen.

That Frank wishes to emphasize this similarity of fates is reflected in the structure of *Cervantes*, which parallels that of Cervantes' *Don Quixote*. In both novels the first of the two parts is filled with the various adventures that reflect hope and despair, love and disappointment, idealism and disillusionment—all the factors that shape the character of Cervantes' Don Quixote and Frank's Cervantes—and closes with the end of the great adventures, marking the end of youth. The second part of each is devoid of great adventures, includes more dialogue and scenes of reflection, and offers greater insight into the characters of Don Quixote and Cervantes.

Frank's duplicating the structure of Cervantes' *Don Quixote* in his own *Cervantes* underscores the parallels in both novels to the lives of Frank and his exiled contemporaries. Frank fled Germany immediately after the Reichstag fire and wrote *Cervantes* during his first period of exile in Switzerland. Both books of Frank's *Cervantes* end with the triumph of freedom: Book I with the physical freedom from slavery in Algiers, Book II with the inner freedom expressed in the writing of *Don Quixote*.[16] For the exiles, too, life was often sharply divided into two parts. The first half, filled with the adventures of youth and experiences in the school of life that alternately renew hope and provoke disillusionment, ends with exile—the triumph of physical freedom. The proverb "Church or sea or courts of kings, / One of these good fortune brings" (30) is no more applicable to the exiles than to Cervantes' Don Quixote or to Frank's Cervantes, for under Nazi domination, religious, military, and political institutions are filled with the same moral corruption that characterizes them in *Don Quixote* and *Cervantes*.

The second half of the exiles' lives becomes, often, a time of sheer survival, of reflection on their past and present—a time, for many, of writing their most valuable literary comments on their lives and age. They shared with Cervantes' Don Quixote and Frank's Cervantes much of the same morality, love of mankind, and sense of justice. Cervantes sought to preserve these qualities and expose the moral corruption of his age in *Don Quixote*. Similarly, Frank and his exiled contemporaries attempted to preserve their cultural tradition and expose the injustice and moral corruption of Nazi Germany, not infrequently through historical novels. Just as Cervantes' Don Quixote becomes a symbol of inner freedom in the face of suppression and suffering, Frank's Cervantes becomes a symbol for the contemporary world in the face of Nazism and exile.

In addition to the parallelism between the structure of Frank's *Cervantes* and Cervantes' *Don Quixote*, there are points of reference between thematic elements in the novel and Frank's contemporary world. Though rarely direct parallels, these references are nevertheless unmistakable.

While there are vast differences, for example, between Philip II and Hitler and between Philip's Spain and Hitler's Germany, Frank's portrayal of Philip and Spain has much to say about Hitler and Germany. Philip is physically decaying through sickness just as Spain is morally decaying under his rule. Hitler, while not physically decaying, presides over and nourishes the moral decay of Germany.

Both Philip and Hitler are obsessed with the idea of world domination, which they pursue blindly despite the resultant exploitation and moral corruption of their people. They see themselves as executors of a divine will, a shared self-delusion, for they are actually the greatest offenders against moral justice and mankind. Both, while believing themselves the embodiment of their people, actually stand diametrically opposed to them.[17]

Philip and Hitler are equally obsessed with the idea of racial purity. They pursue a course of cruelty and inhumanity, one through the Inquisition, the other through the SS. Frank emphasizes the absurdity of the idea of racial purity in Philip's Spain, a country of Iberians, Basques, Celts, Phoenicians, Romans, Vandals, Jews, Goths, Arabs, and Berbers: even its royalty is not racially pure, a fact which forced the adoption of artifical laws of royal succession (254–55). Frank's real concern is, of course, the absurdity of the idea of racial purity in twentieth-century Germany, which receives graphic expression in his presentation of Cervantes' *El retablo de las maravillas* (260–64) and in his portrayal of Cervantes and Gutierrez chanting "Today every ass / For pure-blooded would pass" (264).

Philip's grotesque preoccupation with the dead, vividly symbolized in his construction of the shrine in "The Dead Kings" (100–106), points to his almost cultic association with the past and with decay. Hitler's manipulation of Calliope and Clio to mythologize German history, through which he justifies his own ascendency, reveals a similar preoccupation. Notwithstanding dissimilarities of circumstance and method, both Philip and Hitler minister to death and decay. Calliope and

Clio, however, also collaborate with the exiled author in his evocation of the truth and fate of Hitler and the Germany he rules—a climactic fall evoked by Frank's portrayal of the satanic storm that destroys Philip's shrine and carries the monarch's ornate attire into the mud (105–6).

Similarities between sixteenth-century Spain and twentieth-century Germany also emerge in Frank's portrayal of Catalina's love for courtly novels, particularly the *Amadis* novels. Frank has Cervantes characterize these books as devoid of reality, but they are nevertheless taken for truth, and not only by Catalina. "A whole people clutched in fancy after the impossible" (232) becomes a thinly veiled reference to Germany clinging to the fantasy of lost grandeur and power, a fantasy that allows the nation to avoid confronting the reality of the present.

The portrayal of Spanish super-heroes and pseudo-historical figures of a grand age parallels the Nazi falsification and glorification of Germany's history in order to nourish the Nazi cause and manipulate the thinking of the German people. Frank has Cervantes attempt to replace the Spaniards' fantasy with the reality of his own heroic novel, *The Siege of Numantia*. Its stark reality, particularly the image of the bloodied bread, is perceived by his audience as disgusting and distorted, indicating their inability to comprehend reality when confronted with it (234–36).

Frank's comment as Cervantes leaves Esquivias after this incident—"Words were meaningless" (236)—reflects the plight of Frank and his contemporaries who fled their homeland because their words had become meaningless to the mass of German people. Their attempts inside Germany to draw attention to the reality of Nazism and Hitler were disregarded, disbelieved, or thwarted, and they themselves were scorned, persecuted, and finally forced into exile.

This inability of the masses to see the reality of their own lives is illustrated even more graphically in the closing chapter of the novel, in which Cervantes reads a passage from *Don Quixote* to a group of prisoners (298–300). They shout their approval of the beatings dealt to Don Quixote in return for his aid in freeing a group of prisoners. Angry at first, Cervantes soon realizes that the prisoners are incapable of grasping the reality of their own fates. He vows to provide a key to his novel, one that will reveal the truth to everyone; this key is simply the word "good" (301).

That man is still capable of good in the face of the greatest odds, that man can still preserve his inner freedom against such odds, is the focal point of *Don Quixote,* and Frank makes the same point in *Cervantes.* Sixteenth-century Spain and twentieth-century Germany are worlds turned upside down, where illusion and fantasy distort reality, and where rulers, who should be wise, are madmen, and the truly good and wise are treated as insane. Cervantes and Frank cannot refrain from criticizing and exposing the ages in which they live, but they do not condemn their fellow man completely, for they both possess genuine human sympathy for the plight of their fellow man.[18]

Clearly Frank did not intend *Cervantes* to be a biography. Instead, he made Calliope superior to Clio and converted the historical material surrounding the life of Cervantes into a novel of significance and relevance for his own age. Cervantes wrote *Don Quixote* at the threshold of a new era whose emergence was blocked by tyranny, injustice, and moral corruption. The note of optimism present in the closing of *Cervantes* indicates that Frank sees his own world at a similar threshold; though the path is blocked by Nazi tyranny and the ignorance of the masses, the people can—and must—be educated to the truth.[19] It is to this end that Frank wrote *Cervantes,* the *Don Quixote* of a twentieth-century German exile.

Robert Neumann
The Queen's Doctor

Robert Neumann uses the historical example of Count Johan Frederick Struensee in Denmark to create a parody on politics. In *The Queen's Doctor,*[20] he reveals politics to be composed of the most divergent interests, of the highest and basest instincts of man, and to be often determined by interactions or chain reactions initiated by seemingly unrelated, insignificant events. His parody succeeds not only because it mirrors the politics of his age (and politics in general), but also because it integrates the confusion of elements that comprise national politics with the structural and stylistic elements of the novel.[21] Although Clio provides numerous tiles for this parody puzzle, Calliope pieces them together to form the various patterns which emerge.

The opening paragraph of the novel is not merely geographical description, but a presentation of the major spheres of influence that determine the life and politics of Denmark and a characterization of the main thematic and stylistic elements of the novel: "Where the odd islands and bays of foreign land were not Russian or Prussian they were parts of Brunswick or Hanover, or some other German duchy, and it took an expert knowledge to discriminate among them" (3). The geographical elements refer to political spheres that are in turn represented by the figures of the novel—Christian, Matilda, Juliane, Struensee, Schimmelmann, Bernstorff, Rantzau, Niels Nielsen as representative of the masses, and a host of other minor characters. Though basically in opposition, the spheres of influence align or ally themselves to each other in ever-changing patterns in a constant state of flux and confusion, crystallizing around central points to form highly unstable constellations of power. The formation and dissolution of these relationships is a never-ending process throughout the novel.

The pentapartite structure of the novel incorporates both rigid and dynamic elements. The five books are arranged in a rigid pyramidal structure reminiscent of classical drama. Books I and V portray Struensee in isolation: in Book I as a result of his desire to remain anonymous, in Book V as a result of his imprisonment and execution. Books II and IV portray transitions between power and impotence: Struensee's rise to power in Book II and his fall in Book IV. Book III presents Struensee at the height of his power. The dynamic component reveals itself in the individual books, each of which presents a stage in Struensee's political career, and, at the same time, a new pattern in the constellation of power as the diverse forces crystallize, dissolve, and recrystallize.[22]

The individual scenes, which reflect structurally and stylistically this flux and confusion of elements within the intricate web of political relationships, are not really self-contained episodes that unfold chronologically; rather, they are partial scenes that occur either simultaneously or as a series of seemingly unrelated events. Like the elements of a film mosaic, they assume meaning only when seen in the context of a larger pattern.[23]

The juxtaposition of simultaneous events, as exemplified in Matilda's arrival in and departure from Altona on her way to Copenhagen and the introduction of Struensee into the novel, allows Neumann to draw connections that would otherwise not become evident. By presenting three potential encounters between Struensee and Matilda in Book I, Neumann thematically, structurally, and symbolically renders their initial relationship: they do not know each other, they do not actually meet, they remain isolated from each other, but their potential relationship is firmly established. Berndt, Rantzau (with his relationship to the court of Catherine of Russia), and the philosophy of Rousseau all figure in the course of these potential encounters. By having this combination of elements immediately precede the encounter between Christian and Matilda, which rapidly develops into estrangement, Neumann presents in a very short space some of the most important elements and forces of the novel.

In order to present simultaneous but divergent perspectives and to show the discrepancy between what is and what seems to be, Neumann also juxtaposes outside reports to the narrator's accounts,[24] as illustrated by the series of accounts concerning the Christian-Matilda marriage pact deliberations carried out by Bernstorff for Denmark and Gunning for England. This stylistic technique points beyond individual characterization, for it brings out the selfish political interests of two powers which are so identical that Neumann offers a single final report, using double pronouns, which combines the proposed happiness of the intended pair and the desired deflection of a Danish-French agreement.

Finally, Neumann anchors seemingly unrelated, insignificant events to a single point that, though meaningless in itself, draws the intricate relationship between the various events into focus. One such anchor is the date, January 28, 1771. The series of events drawn together begins with the rise of the prostitute, Anna Katherine Benthaken, from Leggings-Kate to Milady to *Maîtresse en titre* to Baroness von der Rosen. This rise parallels the deteriorating relations between Christian and Matilda. The virtual rape of Matilda by Christian to produce an heir to the throne, the death of Holck's child bride, the chaotic incident in the "Green Café," and Christian's hasty decision to travel (i.e., to flee from Denmark), all occur on January 28. This confusion of events anchored on a single date serves to point out the interconnections among Christian's relationship with Matilda, his flight from duty and irresponsible mode of living, his exorbitant waste, the plight of the masses, and the role of prostitution in politics, literally and figuratively.

Superimposed on the rigid pyramidal structure of the books and the film mosaic of the individual scenes is a cyclical structure composed of a series of thematic elements that connect Books I and V. Political confusion and instability, the political marriage arrangements between Christian and Matilda as they are initiated and dissolved, the figure of Rousseau and Rousseauistic reforms, and the introduction and execution of Struensee bring these elements full circle.

The most important symbolic element in this cyclical structure is the medallion Struensee picks up from the dance floor in England in Book I and rediscovers in his pocket as he is dressing for his execution in Book V. This medallion "was a worthless thing on a cheap chain, and the head of an unknown woman was painted on it; the painting was slick and smooth and unreal, so that one could not tell if it were an imaginary head or a botched attempt at a portrait. Struensee balanced it on his palm and decided that it was at least sufficiently related to life not to merit being cast back among the rubbish" (74–75). This symbolizes the course of Struensee's life, the political power that fate placed into his hand, and the uncertainty of the reality and value of both. By keeping the medallion in England and replacing it in his pocket before his execution, Struensee affirms the course of his life and his actions.

Among the many thematic elements in the novel, four emerge with particular importance: the role of the individualistic outsider within society, the position of the Jew in society and politics, the relationship between money and politics, and the relationship between the masses and those in power. Each of these elements refers, directly or indirectly, to Neumann's contemporary world.[25]

Struensee and Schimmelmann exemplify the role of the individualistic outsider. Struensee, a middle-class doctor from Altona filled with Rousseauistic reform ideas, literally and figuratively comes from a different world. When he enters the circle of royalty in Copenhagen, where Rousseau is virtually unknown, he becomes a type of fool and dreamer, a doctor who wants to cure the sickness and insanity of the Danish court.

Schimmelmann not only presents the role of the Jew in society and politics but also serves as the stereotype traditionally assigned to the Jew by non-Jews in a non-Jewish society. Schimmelmann's appraisal of non-Jews—"It never dawns on them that a Jew simply has to acquire a name and a great fortune to keep himself from being burnt at the stake" (64)—demonstrates that he suffers no illusions concerning the attitudes of non-Jews toward his position in society. The attitude of non-Jews towards Jews is revealed by Bernstorff and Keith—both pragmatic and relatively positive figures—to be a mixture of hatred and envy that reflects a traditional anti-Semitic mentality, particularly that of the German masses in the early 1930s. Jews became the scapegoats for all political and economic shortcomings in society and government. The source of this hate-envy, which normalizes as necessitated tolerance in the case of Bernstorff and Keith, is the dependence of the State (Struensee) on the financial élan of the Jew (Schimmelmann). This dependence, however, evolves into a vendetta against both, for Struensee comes to be viewed as having sold out the interests of Denmark to "Jewish financiers and Jewish profiteers" (300).

Struensee represented a ray of hope for the Jews. He had initiated freedom of the press, emancipation, and the dissolution of the ghettos so that Jews could fully integrate into society. This hope, however, is combined with a sense of foreboding, symbolized in the portrait of Struensee, Matilda, and Sigmund Schimmelmann painted at the height of Struensee's power. The narrator comments on the painting: "We are still smiling, [which] means, we are still breathing, we are still involved in countless things and shall not die" (213). By using the pronoun "we," Neumann comments directly about himself, his contemporaries, and Germany. In all cases, this ominous feeling is fully justified: Struensee rejects Schimmelmann's plea for a rational fiscal policy in favor of an easy answer to the State's financial problems, the lottery; for Germany, a far worse horror looms in the future—the mass exterminations of Jews.

It is in connection with the lottery that the contrast between the outsider, Schimmelmann, and the majority is revealed with clarity and grotesque humor, as the frenzy of closing trading during the stock market incident assumes the character of a zoological nightmare.[26] Schimmelmann clearly sees the ramifications of Struensee's decision in favor of the lottery but assumes a stoic attitude towards the fate of the Jews: "A pity, he thought. A pity for lots of reasons. That man wanted to establish liberty, he thought, as if he were thinking of a dead man. Liberty—and now it had all ended in a banal Prussian lottery. A pity. But Baron Schimmelmann belonged to a people who had used the expression 'A pity' a great number of times in the last few thousand years" (217). The results of Struensee's decision culminate on the day of the stock market incident with the incitement against the Jews, the attack on Struensee, and the mob violence against the Jews in the Jewish quarter. The ultimate results are the fall and execution of Struensee and the death of Sigmund.

In the marriage arrangements worked out by Gunning and Bernstorff, the relationship between money and politics is immediately apparent. They prompt the union between Christian and Matilda and attend the dissolution of the marriage. The initial refusal of Denmark to return the dowry to England and the scandal created by the divorce of Christian and Matilda ultimately result in England's attack on Denmark years later. Christian and Matilda are thus mere objects of price haggling, pawns in an international chess game of power alliances.

Christian's extravagant wastefulness during his travels to England and France gives a clear picture of his insanity and ineptitude as a monarch. It also gives rise to his direct connection to Schimmelman: After draining the finances of his nation, the king literally pawns his country to Schimmelman, who funds Christian's travels, saves the lottery stocks, provides the funds to repay the dowry, and ends up owning all the royal possessions of Denmark.

Niels Nielsen represents the masses in their relationship to those in power. Although life under the monarchy is wretched, the people remain passive, afraid to disturb the recognized authority that provides an established order for their existence. Struensee challenges that order and destroys the admittedly corrupt regime upon which it is based, but he fails to replace it with a viable new order. Caught in the middle, the masses are left feeling insecure, and their relationship to those in power becomes one of wavering loyalties and fickleness. The shifts in their position can be seen in Niels, who undergoes a transformation in the course of the novel from a passive sufferer under the old monarchy to a fanatical supporter of Struensee. Eventually, however, the instability of Struensee's authority leads Niels to transfer his loyalty back to Christian; in the end, Niels serves as Struensee's executioner.

These thematic elements clearly reveal parallels between the historical material of the novel and Neumann's contemporary world.[27] The masses, who in executing Struensee symbolically destroy the Rousseauistic political reforms that Struensee attempted to initiate on their behalf, are motivated by greed, are manipulated by mass psychology, are turned against the Jews, and are the mere tools of political powers which they cannot comprehend. Their portrayal could serve as a portrayal of Germany in the early 1930s.[28] The same can be said of the outsider, i.e., those with a political or intellectual orientation opposed to the advent of Nazism into the society and politics of Germany in Neumann's age. Such is the position of the Jew, and even Schimmelmann's horrible insight, "that a Jew simply has to acquire a name and a great fortune to keep himself from being burnt at the stake" (64), proved to be overly optimistic.

Although The Queen's Doctor presents historical material directly and to a certain extent factually, it does not do so for the sake of history. Far from being a mere fictionalized biography of Struensee and a historical account of his age, the novel becomes a literary expression of politics in general, a parody on politics based upon a historical example.[29] As such, it is not limited to a particular geographical area or historical period, but has general significance as well, as demonstrated by the unmistakable references to Newmann's contemporary world.[30]

Edgar Maass
Don Pedro and the Devil

Edgar Maass' *Don Pedro and the Devil*[31] is a multifaceted historical novel set in an age of massive political and religious upheaval, an era caught between the twilight of the Old World and the dawning of the New. This turning point is marked by the collapse of the last vestiges of knightly ideals under the realities and demands of a new age in which gold is mistaken for God and Christian ideals are diametrically opposed to the actions of the church. All this, however, merely reflects the inner turmoil of man himself.

Against the background of sixteenth-century Spain and Peru, Maass brings these themes to life through vividly portrayed adventures and personalities. Bartolomé de Las Casas, Agrippa of Nettesheim, Joanna the Mad, Charles V, the Pizarro brothers, Pater Vicente de Valverde, Atahualpa, Loyola, de Soto, and Cortés are all depicted, albeit with varying degrees of factualness; Maass takes obvious pleasure in allying himself with Clio as long as the historical material suits the purposes dictated by Calliope.

Beyond this historical material, however, is the more profound content of the novel revealed through the first person account of Don Pedro de Cordova, a young man caught up in the turmoil of his age.[32] This account, which refers in many respects to Maass' contemporary world, is the personal confession of a sinner who finds his way back to God. As such, the novel unmistakably presents a Parsifal account in a Spanish setting, for it traces the life of Don Pedro, who was orphaned as a baby and raised by a nurse and servant, from the state of ignorance and innocence, into the depths of sin and guilt, to final redemption in the knowledge of God's truth.[33]

Love and innocence initially lead Don Pedro into a state of sin. His love for Isabella, the childhood sweetheart for whom he promised to conquer a kingdom, his love for Agrippa and

Abu Amru, which brings him into conflict with the Inquisition for refusing to betray them, and his love and sense of Christian duty towards Queen Joanna, who orders him to go to the New World bearing the cross of Christ—these are the motivating factors which cause Don Pedro to join a group of vagabonds and accompany the Pizarros on their voyage to the New World.

Don Pedro's fall into sin results from mistaking the true path to God. He initially believes he is serving God by conquering the outer world—a belief supported by the teaching of Agrippa and the order of Queen Joanna—rather than the inner world of his own soul. His most serious sin, however, is one of omission, his failure to follow an inner voice of compassion, his passive affirmation of murder and plundering.

After the arrival in the New World, Don Pedro begins to sense the nature of the Pizarros' undertaking—one which is opposed to its avowed Christian purpose—but he does not realize the consequences for his own soul. Maass portrays the fall into sin and guilt with an intensity and an increasing tension. As Don Pedro's difficulties and disappointments mount during his journey up the Andes toward his desired goal, the capital of Atahualpa, so does the lust for blood and gold and the distance between the supposed Christian undertaking and its true nature. The ascent of the Andes symbolizes, in effect, a descent into hell, the fall into sin for Don Pedro. At the very height of worldly conquest on the peaks of the Andes, Don Pedro commits his greatest sin, the passive betrayal of Atahualpa.

Don Pedro, however, does not become conscious of his sins until he returns to Spain and is rejected by everyone, including Isabella, for his part in the plundering of the Incan treasures for personal gain and the betrayal and murder of Atahualpa. In a state of despair and self-loathing, he withdraws from the world, believing his sins too great to be forgiven.

Through a dream and the decisive encounter with Las Casas before Charles V, in which Don Pedro confesses his guilt and thus cleanses his soul, he finds his way back to God. This confession, this active dedication of his life to Christ on behalf of the Indians, is the real sign of Don Pedro's attainment of the Holy Grail. The jousting contest between Don Pedro and Molina, by which the fate of the Indians in the New World will be decided, is a contrived attempt to complete the Parsifal theme and symbolize the attainment of the Holy Grail.

Despite this weakness, the Parsifal theme is maintained throughout the novel. The main point of this theme, that the Holy Grail can only be attained by passing through and overcoming the depths of sin and recognizing the true relationship between God and the world, is clearly indicated in the words of Las Casas: "'Lord, lead us into temptation that we may find you! Let us sink up to our necks in evil, so that we may know you! Let us suck dry the gall of disbelief, that we may learn faith!'" (320–21).

The novel closes with a children's game which also symbolizes the Parsifal theme. A blindfolded child, who tries to capture a lighted candle, stands in a circle of children who pass the candle among themselves and sing:

> "Is the little light here?
> No, it's there, over there.
> Is the little light here?
> Might be there, anywhere.
> Have you got the light?
> Just think a bit faster!
> Come tell, where's the light!
> It's in God, in the Master!"   [634]

Man's universal search for God and for the ultimate truth within himself is the path which Don Pedro has trodden.

Although the Parsifal aspect of the novel is presented mainly through thematic elements, the structure of the novel also supports it. The novel begins in Spain, depicting Don Pedro as an innocent youth who naively embarks on the path which leads to sin. It then moves to the New World, which marks his actual fall into sin and guilt. Finally, it returns to Spain, a shift which signifies Don Pedro's consciousness of his sins, his desire for forgiveness, and his attainment of the Holy Grail.

In support of the Parsifal theme, Don Pedro's fall from and return to God is marked by a series of teachers. His first is Agrippa of Nettesheim, who teaches him to read and write, introduces him to the Bible, and initiates him into his own endeavors as an alchemist. Alchemy is one of the many factors that lead Don Pedro away from God, for Agrippa is trying to find God by discovering the ultimate element of the universe, the *Quinta essentia*, through the material world, namely, through gold. These two characters follow parallel paths: Both seek God—Don Pedro through action in the material world, Agrippa through science—and both are brought to the ultimate realization of their sin by Las Casas.

Queen Joanna is a mother figure whom Don Pedro sees as the mother of all Spain as well as a counterpart to the Mother of God. Another of Don Pedro's teachers, she sets a moral example for him. She is known by everyone as "Joanna the Mad," but the Spanish people qualify her insanity by adding: "mad with love" (74). She is the only person who could effect a settlement of the political turmoil between the Comuneros and her son, Charles V, but she loves all of Spain and could not betray one for the sake of the other. Her command to Don Pedro to go to the New World bearing the cross of Christ has paradoxical import. Don Pedro, of course, believes that to be his true mission when he sets out for the New World, but he soon realizes the truth once he arrives. In the end, however, his voyage to the New World does indeed represent the cross of Christ which he must bear.

Abu Amru bin Al-Jad, whom Don Pedro meets through Agrippa, also has moral and spiritual lessons to offer Don Pedro, but they fail to permeate his consciousness. The dichotomy of gold versus God is present in the figures of Agrippa and Abu Amru, for Abu Amru tries unsuccessfully to convince Agrippa that finding the *Quinta essentia* depends on the nature of the search and that seeking the ultimate element of the universe in gold represents a misdirected approach.

Inigo Lopez de Recalde represents a Parsifal model for Don Pedro, but since the encounter takes place while Don Pedro is still in a state of ignorance and innocence, he fails to grasp the lesson Inigo has to offer. Inigo calls himself a student, one who has had war, sickness, death, and despair as his teachers. Inigo sees in Don Pedro's plan to go to the New World the spectre of his own life repeated, and he therefore warns Don Pedro that " 'the true crusade is not a question of geographical length and width, but of spiritual depth. Dark forests lie in our own hearts. Man himself is a Nova Terra' " (202).

Atahualpa, the figure most closely associated with Don Pedro's fall into sin, proves to be one of Don Pedro's most significant teachers, for through him Don Pedro becomes aware of his inner self. Although Atahualpa does not understand why Spaniards are so greedy for gold, it is he who interprets for Don Pedro the effect gold actually has on the soul of man. His admonition—"'you people are not children of light, but children of gold'" (444)—not only contrasts the Incan and the Spanish concepts of gold, but also reveals how gold, sought and used in the manner of the Spaniards, enslaves man. Such a contrast is also revealed in regard to Christianity. Though viewed by the church as an idol-worshipping heathen who knows nothing about Christianity and the Bible, it is Atahualpa who makes Don Pedro aware of the hollowness of his own Christianity.

This contrast is portrayed with grotesque cruelty but historical factualness in the baptism and execution of Atahualpa. On the night following the celebration of John the Baptist, Atahualpa is baptized by Pater Vicente, absolving him of all sins before God. This is the same priest who earlier stressed the Christian duty of extorting the Incan gold at any price, however, and his religion does not prompt him to object to the execution of Atahualpa following the baptism; "'secular justice is outside my province'" (511), he rationalizes. Don Pedro witnesses both acts but stands by unable to speak or act; his deafness towards his inner voice protesting these acts constitutes his sin of omission.

It is through Las Casas that Don Pedro ultimately finds his way back to God. The relationship between Las Casas and Don Pedro reflects Don Pedro's growing awareness of his inner voice. His first encounter with Las Casas, which occurs before the voyage to the New World, is in fact a third-hand account of the man in a letter from Agrippa. Don Pedro thus knows of Las Casas' existence, but fails to see any connection to his own life, just as he fails to comprehend what his inner voice is trying to tell him. The second encounter takes place in the jungles of the New World, but Don Pedro does not know that the man before him is Las Casas, who contrasts the purported and the true mission of the Conquistadores, showing the paradoxical stand of Christianity. The third and decisive encounter takes place in connection with Las Casas' appearance before Charles V to plead for the freedom of the Indians and an end to slavery and massacre in the New World. The spiritual sickness of Spain is reflected in this climactic audience, where Sepulveda and Molina argue in favor of continuing the rape of the New World, Loyola and Las Casas argue for the freedom of the Indians and their equal treatment as Spanish subjects, and the Grand Inquisitor argues for a regulated slavery, one which protects certain material rights but which offers the security which he sees the Indians desiring more than their freedom. Don Pedro, in an act of self-purification, openly confesses his guilt before the king for his role in the plundering of Incan cities, the massacre of the citizens, and the betrayal and murder of Atahualpa, thus giving weight to Las Casas' argument. This act represents for Don Pedro the ultimate comprehension of his inner voice, for he now dedicates his life to serving Christ.

Don Pedro's path from innocence, through sin, and back to God is foretold and accompanied by a series of dreams: the childhood dream in which the devil appears to him and almost crushes him with gold pieces; the dream in the New World in which the helmet of Don Francisco Pizarro presses so hard against his temples that his head almost bursts; the dream prior to the execution of Atahualpa in which the Grand Inquisitor comes at Don Pedro with a black crucifix and then attempts to strangle him; and the final dream, after the rejection by Isabella, in which a hooded figure appears claiming to be a surgeon, one who cannot heal but can expose tumors or peel back the skin to reveal the cause of sickness.

With one exception, all of these dreams are followed by a figure who is or represents the Virgin Mary, a symbolic indication that Don Pedro will ultimately atone for his sins and attain the Holy Grail. Significantly, the dream that precedes the execution of Atahualpa does not end with such a figure, for from that point to the final dream, Don Pedro considers his sin too great to be forgiven. The final dream, however, represents Don Pedro's full consciousness and acknowledgement of his sins, and his desire for and realization of the possibility of atonement.

In order to emphasize the inherent paradox of the Parsifal theme—that the path to God and self-realization leads through sin—Maass employs numerous contrasts: good and evil, the spiritual and the worldly, the inner and the outer self, God and gold. Even the most peripheral figures and incidents are utilized to create a paradox within a paradox. The mummer figure of the devil, for example, is the husband of the figure of the Holy Virgin, but the words of the devil figure actually destroy the outward contrast between the devil and the Holy Virgin and thus place the devil figure in contrast to himself.

The figures of Agrippa and Abu Amru, which contrast gold with God, the worldly with the spiritual; the words of Inigo, which contrast the geographical with the inner Nova Terra; and the baptism and execution of Atahualpa are further examples which have already been treated. These contrasts are even reflected in the name of the ship, the *Espiritu Santo*, that bears the Pizarros and Don Pedro to the New World. It is in the words of the Grand Inquisitor and Pater Vicente, however, that the contrasts are especially evident.

When Don Pedro appears before the Inquisition, the Grand Inquisitor admonishes him to choose between the voice of the church and the voice Don Pedro senses within himself. The Grand Inquisitor interprets this inner voice as saying: " 'that any heaven on earth which shows the smallest crack in its foundations is not Heaven, but the kingdom of lies. It is Hell itself. . . . Decide for yourself, my son . . . to whom you will hearken. To the Voice of God, who speaks through our Holy Mother the Roman Catholic Church and through the Holy Inquisition, or to the voice whispering within your own heart' " (130–31). The Grand Inquisitor's characterization of Don Pedro's inner voice is what the Grand Inquisitor and the church actually represent, whereas the truth of the inner voice is that which the Grand Inquisitor and the church believe they represent but do not.

These contrastual elements are carried to a grotesque extreme in the figure of Pater Vicente. The paradox of his words to Atahualpa is self-evident: " 'We have come to this land to save you and all these thousands of Indians from a terrible fate. We have come to offer you the teachings of Christ' " (426). Similarly, he justifies the extortion of Atahualpa's treasure as a work pleasing to God while disclaiming any interest in temporal, political matters, but then immediately proceeds to outline a military plan aimed at pitting Atahualpa against his half-brother, Huáscar, thus destroying the Incan Empire. This contrast is carried to its outer limits when he openly advocates murdering Atahualpa should all else fail.

These contrastual elements, which support and emphasize the seeming paradox of the Parsifal theme, also support the direct references to the contemporary world which Maass draws from the historical material.[35] Maass' world is one of war, destruction, and moral decay, all of which are reflected in the political turmoil in Spain and the devastation wrought in the New World.[36] These elements assume apocalyptic dimensions in the vision of Queen Joanna: " 'I see dark drawing over the earth. Brothers will murder one another. Parents will deny their children, children their elders. They will throw themselves down before Baal and pray to false gods. I see uprisings, war, hunger and misery' " (193). Her vision offers a scarcely veiled reference to the programmed moral depravity of the Nazi period. Similarly, Agrippa's call for a different kind of war against the true heathens—by which he means not the Indians but rather the Spaniards, " 'the good Catholics who pray to the gods of gold, force, betrayal and cruelty, whose bellies are big as casks with wickedness' " (569)—and Las Casas' concern for the soul of Spain whose cruelty towards the Indians has become a thorn in the flesh of conscience (584–85) are in fact references to the moral decay and anti-Semitism inside Nazi Germany.

Attendant on this moral decay is the twisting of justice, first revealed in the methods the Inquisition uses in attempting to force false testimony and confessions from Don Pedro and Abu Amru, methods which result in the torture and death of Abu Amru. A similar travesty of justice is portrayed in the trial of Atahualpa, for the charges brought against him are without basis and are proven, through logic, to be false. Since the trial does not actually concern his guilt or innocence, but is merely the irrational means to an end, nonreason prevails and Atahualpa is executed. Both of these incidents reflect the prevailing code of ethics, or the total lack of one, in the Nazi judicial system.

One of the most frequent Nazi justifications for war was the need to expand the German "Lebensraum." Sepulveda argues along the same lines, claiming that Spain must conquer and subdue the Indians in order to insure its own prosperity. For him, there is no alternative, for " 'the Spaniards in the New World would grow poor and die of hunger. For what can nourish them, if not the labor of the Indians?' " (582).

Racism is dealt with numerous times in the novel. The idea of a Master Race is vividly portrayed, again in the words of Sepulveda: " 'There is not the slightest doubt that the Indians are an inferior people, doomed to slavery, and that on the other hand the Spaniards are a ruling people, born to command. It is not only the right, it is moreover the duty of Spain to rule the Indians, to force them to work, and to kill them should they presume to question the superiority of us Spaniards' " (580–81). The content, choice of words, and mentality behind this statement are mirrored in the speeches of Hitler and Goebbels.

A more direct reference in the novel to the German attitude towards the Jews is revealed in the Spanish attitude towards the Moors. These are the very people to whom Spain is indebted for much of its culture and its finest products. The racist attitude towards the Moors proves to be based on envy of their history, skill, and industry. Persecution or forced exile, the choice of the Jews and many intellectuals in Nazi Germany— insofar as they could exercise a choice—is the choice which confronts the Moors and Free Thinkers in Spain under the programmed persecution initiated by Charles V. Abu Amru succumbs to persecution, but Agrippa finds exile in Flanders, and Don Pedro escapes to the New World, the main refuge for the exiled Germans fleeing the persecution of Nazi Germany.

The mass extermination of the Jews in Nazi Germany finds reference in Las Casas' description of the fate of the Indians at the hands of the Spaniards: " 'Fifty years ago there were two million people alive on Hispaniola. Today there are scarcely five hundred suffering creatures left. Where have they gone? Have they all flown away to some other place? No, they have been slaughtered like cattle, torn apart and burned at the stake' " (590). As Las Casas continues, the horrors committed in Nazi concentration camps are paralleled, not in specific methods and pictures, but in corresponding methodology and imagery: " 'I have seen screaming infants tossed into the fire for sport. I have seen hundreds of men imprisoned in three small houses—men, women and children. . . . The Spaniards set the houses on fire and burned the contents to a mass of char. . . . Thousands of Indians die of overwork. And these are considered lucky by their Indian fellows, for the Spaniards have long since turned the Carib paradise into a hell from which death is a desperately sought for release' " (591).

Maass never allows these direct references to become direct parallels. They are a natural part of the historical material and are fully integrated into the Parsifal theme created from it. The result is that they never overwhelm the material at the expense of the novel as a whole, but are nevertheless always conscious in the reader's mind. The integration of the three levels of expression—the historical material itself, the Parsifal theme, and the references to the contemporary world in connection with both—makes *Don Pedro and the Devil* a contemporary literary expression of unmistakable merit.

Lion Feuchtwanger
The Pretender

Although *The Pretender*[37] must be counted as one of Lion Feuchtwanger's weakest works, it merits discussion within the context of the historical novel in exile. It points out not only the limitations of this most prolific writer of historical novels among the German exiles, but also the limitations of drawing direct parallels between historical material and the contemporary world in an attempt to parody that world. Intending to illuminate some of the conditions under which Hitler rose to power and the manifestations, consequences, and evil embodied in that power, Feuchtwanger fictionalizes the rise and fall of Terentius Maximus, a man from Asia Minor who, during the reign of Titus, generated a following for a short time by claiming to be Nero. This claim was made believable by his physical features and his voice, both of which strongly resembled those of the dead Nero. The main intent, however, is to mock Hitler and the Nazis, in the hope that such mockery will contribute to the fall of Hitler.

Within the framework of this parody, the novel assumes the characteristics of world drama turned to farce.[38] Structurally the parody is enhanced by the novel's division into four books, each with many short chapters. This, as well as the titles of the four books—"Rise," "Triumph," "Decline," and "Fall"—reflects a pyramidal dramatic structure of four acts, each with many short scenes. Varro writes the script and sets the stage for a drama which contains the elements of petty revenge and the ambitious synthesis of East and West. He loses control over his own creation, however: new actors appear and change the script, turning the planned world drama into a tragic farce in which the actors so completely identify with their roles that they lose touch with reality.

In effect, the novel becomes a double farce: in setting the stage and manipulating the characters to parody the contemporary scene, Feuchtwanger allows the actors to assume a variety of often contradictory roles and draws such exaggerated parallels between his fictionalized figures and contemporary figures that the effectiveness of the parody is destroyed.

The main actors in this farce are Varro, Terence, Knops, Trebanius, and John of Patmos. The triumvirate Terence-Knops-Trebanius and its later manifestation as "The Three-Headed Monster" are transparent references to the Nazi triumvirate Hitler-Goebbels-Goering. Knops, however, also assumes traits of Goering, and both Knops and Trebanius assume traits of Ernst Röhm.[39] John of Patmos is associated with figures and events ranging from Georgi Dimitroff and Thomas Mann to Feuchtwanger himself. The treatment of Titus, although he is barely mentioned, alludes to the ailing Hindenburg. Varro is an unclear mixture of conflicting elements: in part a representative of the German people as a whole, in part a representative of German big business in support of Nazism, in part Feuchtwanger.

Terence—a potter of questionable ability, a devotee of the theater and monumental architecture, and a captivating speaker—is the only character consistently associated with a single figure, that of Hitler. The fact that little serious attention was paid to Hitler when he first appeared on the political scene in Germany is parodied and Hitler is mocked in the description of Terence when he first arrived in Edessa: "At that time he looked like some common fellow whom one would expect to wipe his nose with his elbow, like the Greek worker of the proverb. Nobody could have foretold in that Terence the future master of the guild" (18). Just as Terence becomes obsessed with the idea that he really is Nero, Hitler believed himself to be the incarnation of the "Zeitgeist." And like Hitler, Terence-Nero is portrayed as the Anti-Christ.

Although various factors motivate Varro to create Nero out of Terence, it is basically a mixture of personal vendetta against Cejonius and grandiose visions of world empire—a union of East and West—which induces Varro to take action. As a representative and spokesman for the German people as a whole, Varro's personal vendetta reflects the bitterness and humiliation of the German people in response to the harsh reparations imposed on them in the Treaty of Versailles.[40] Cejonius, as representative of Roman power, offers parallels to the victorius powers of the West. These elements are alluded to when Varro tells Cejonius that " 'things aren't going well with the people in Edessa. They have to pay high taxes, they could only gain by a change of government. If a man were to appear and announce that he would abolish their taxes, he'd find a credulous hearing everywhere beyond the Euphrates' " (97).

Varro's identification with Germany and the factions which brought Hitler to power is emphasized through repeated mention of the fact that a need for a Terence-Nero figure precedes his existence, that he must be created, that he exists only through the belief in his existence. Feuchtwanger has Varro lose control over his creation, just as he sees Germany and the powers that created Hitler losing control over him. Terence-Nero turns against Varro just as Hitler, to a certain degree, turned against big business.[41] Varro's reaction, and supposedly that of Germany, is angry impotence and fatalistic resignation, for "he would have liked to get hold of the fellow and strangle him. The position was grotesquely ironical; all that he possessed was bound up with this fellow, and if he destroyed him he would destroy himself" (330).

In these instances, the parallels between Varro and Germany and the powers which contributed to the rise of Hitler are unmistakable. In other instances, however, such parallels lose validity. Varro, for example, regrets the outcome of his actions but still believes in the correctness and rationality underlying them. This indeed reflects the rationale of those who supported Hitler and Nazism. There is, of course, some merit in his idea—here he represents Feuchtwanger's own theories—of uniting East and West for the benefit of both. The unfortunate conclusion he draws from his action, however, namely that in spite of everything, he has made a positive contribution toward that end, can only confuse any association made between Varro and Germany and between his actions and those of the Nazi supporters, for this union of East and West has nothing in common with Hitler's idea of expansionism and the creation of "Lebensraum." This could be accepted and dismissed as tragic self-deception were it not for the end of the novel, in which Feuchtwanger speaks through John of Patmos and praises the positive effects of evil, thus precluding such an interpretation.

The Reichstag fire, the role of the SA in the persecution of Communists and other enemies of the party, the Nazi Boxheimer Document, and the trial and acquittal of Communist Georgi Dimitroff are all parodied in the flooding of the temple of Apamea and its aftermath. The Nazis, by setting fire to the Reichstag and blaming the Communists, hoped to discredit the Communists and win popular support. Knops, here a parody of Goebbels, fabricates the plan to flood Apamea in order to turn the people against John of Patmos and the Christians and win support for Nero. The methods of Goebbel's Propaganda Ministry are reflected in the exchange between Varro and Knops, in which the Apamea plan is first discussed: " 'Aren't you laying it on a little bit thick, my dear Knops?' 'Of course I am laying it on thick, my Varro. . . . But that is the very point of the business, to lay it on thick. The more outrageous a lie is, the more certain it is to be believed'" (200). The big lie as the most effective propaganda method not only alludes to Goebbel's methods but directly to the source of this idea, *Mein Kampf*.[42]

In the chapter "The Night of the Fifteenth of May," Feuchtwanger parallels the events of the Röhm-Putsch (30 June 1934), in which Ernst Röhm, head of the SA, and other high officials in the SA were executed as enemies of Hitler in a wave of terror without trial. The planning of his purge in the novel shows a parallel between Terence-Nero's relationship to Knops and Hitler's relationship to Röhm, except that Terence-Nero does not carry out his plan of eliminating Knops. Included in this parallel is the fate of the potter, Alkas, who was on the list of those to be executed. Trebanius' men mistakenly execute Alkas, the musician, an incident which parallels the execution of Dr. Willi Schmid, an eminent music critic in Munich, mistaken for Willi Schmidt, a local SA leader. The parallels end here, however, for this mass terror did not effectively break the power of Hitler as it helps break the power of Terence-Nero.

John of Patmos' recitation of "Octavia" in the Odeon of Edessa parallels an incident involving a speech Thomas Mann gave in Berlin on 17 October 1930. Just as Mann issued an appeal to reason in dealing with Hitler and Nazism, "Octavia" presents a strong attack on Terence-Nero. The disruption of Mann's speech by a group of NS troops under the leadership of Arnolt Bronnen is paralleled by the disruptions following John's recitation, led by followers of Terence-Nero.

In addition to the parallels drawn between John of Patmos and Dimitroff and Thomas Mann, there are other parallels which point to Feuchtwanger. One of these is the incident in which John's house is ransacked, his books destroyed, and his son beaten. This alludes to the events of early March 1933, when the SA forced their way into Feuchtwanger's villa in Grunewald hoping to arrest him, but, finding that he had not returned from a tour of the United States, beat the porter and plundered the contents of the house.[43]

A parallel of greater significance is found in the chapter "Vanity of Vanities," although it is difficult to say to what extent Feuchtwanger realized he was portraying himself and his novel through his utterances concerning John of Patmos. Like Feuchtwanger, who had escaped the Nazis, John of Patmos is saved from execution and reflects on his fate: "It was a sign. It was God's will that he should live, that he should write down the visions of that night and go about the world proclaiming them. Was there not a little of the actor in every prophet? God had made him an actor with a touch of the prophet. He had reached the stage now where the actor could at last prophesy. John recognized his mission" (229–30). Feuchtwanger was convinced of his abilities as a writer and above all of his great insight into the world and his mission to enlighten others to this insight.[44] Apart from legitimacy in this self-appraisal of Feuchtwanger, he reveals his own impotence in carrying out his mission. John of Patmos' liberator requests that he recite the speech of Oedipus one last time before John goes into exile, but, just as John finds it impossible to practice his art in the face of the immediacy and intensity of the events surrounding him, Feuchtwanger is unable to bridge the gap between the historical situation of his day and artistic expression.

There is no question that Feuchtwanger creates a parody of Hitler and Nazism, but it is one which has only partial validity. At the base of this lies perhaps the fact that, rather than drawing subtle references from historical material which significantly reflect the contemporary world, Feuchtwanger forces contemporary figures and events onto sparse historical material.[45] It is also a handicap that the historical material Feuchtwanger chooses actually has little in common with the contemporary figures and events he parodies. He tries to make this forced identification of the past with the present more believable by quoting, as a preface to the novel, from Ecclesiastes 1:9–11: "The thing that hath been, it is that which shall be; and that which is done is that which shall be done; and there is no new thing under the sun."

That historical patterns repeat themselves may be valid, but applying this idea too literally leads in this case to invalid parallels. Terence-Nero is pictured as a relatively sympathetic figure, a victim of his own mental aberrations and of the exploitation of others, worthy even of sympathetic veneration after death. This can hardly be applied to Hitler. In addition, the portrayal of the main supports of Terence-Nero's rule—Varro, King Mallukh, King Philip, King Artaban, and the priest Scharbil—as representing genuine supranationalism and the mutually beneficial union of East and West as opposed to the nationalistic Flavians is highly curious, for the exact opposite would be expected if this were to apply to Hitler and Nazi Germany. The emphasis placed on the Potter's Song, which mocks Terence-Nero, as one of the major contributing factors in his fall is equally curious. Although the power of such mockery is believable in the historical context of the age of Terence-Nero, the parallel drawn in the novel reflects a naïve expectation that such mockery would ultimately lead to the fall of Hitler.[46]

Thematic and stylistic weaknesses of a more general nature also question this novel's literary value. The major figures in the novel seem to come from the same basic mold. Varro, Cejonius, Knops, Terence, Trebanius, and Marcia all feel that life has been unfair to them, that outside forces have prevented them from realizing their inherent potential. They all place their lives or ideals in jeopardy to compensate for this disadvantage. The contrasts between and within characters are stark and exaggerated: the love-hate feelings between Marcia and Varro and between Varro and Cejonius, for example, seem contrived. The dramatic encounters and visibly constructed intricacies of intrigue, especially in the case of Varro, seem artificial. There is no subtlety of expression or presentation: Feuchtwanger leaves nothing to chance in the interpretation of characters' words or actions. The stock word "reason" becomes a meaningless cliché in the context of the novel. The balance sheet kept by Varro, intended to reflect the consequences of his actions, is also a contrived device. The inclusion of comments on the historical sources is pedantic and out of place. Readers are totally unprepared for the introduction of Claudia Acta. The sudden profession of the love Varro has always felt for Claudia is ludicrous. The amount of space devoted to the arrest, public mockery, and crucifixion of Knops, Terence, and Trebanius, and the obvious pleasure taken in portraying their suffering seem sensational and theatrical, as are the appearance and comforting words of John of Patmos to Knops on the cross.[47]

These elements cannot be accepted as valid literary supports for the dramatic structure of the novel or for the idea of world drama turned to farce. The Pretender must be judged as a novel. The dramatic structure should not be overemphasized, for it serves mainly as a physical division of the material.

At best, this parody is an impotent striking out from a relatively safe distance against forces which Feuchtwanger does not fully understand and for which he has no other means of attack. He expresses spontaneous feelings of hatred toward Hitler and Nazism without effectively dealing with the total historical situation and the mass psychology behind the rise of Hitler.[48] This omission leaves the impression that Feuchtwanger simply accepts as fact that people can be deceived from time to time by the greatest of demagogues regardless of the historical circumstances.[49] This venting of anger undoubtedly brought a certain grim satisfaction for Feuchtwanger as well as for a wide audience, for it allowed in fiction, at least, the exposure and destruction of the hated adversary. This, how-ever, combined with the idea expressed in the last chapter, "He Too Serves Reason," can hardly be considered an effective approach for countering Nazism.

Feuchtwanger's firm belief in the powers of reason and his belief that the greatest evil ultimately serves the powers of reason can be accepted as legitimate,[50] but not in the simplistic terms and the specific context of this novel. Feuchtwanger's naïveté regarding the historical situation of his own day is seen in his assessment of Terence-Nero's outcome and the outcome he envisions for Hitler and Nazism: "The people who sup-ported the wretch Terence had wished to unite the two halves of the world for their common and ignoble ends; but all that remained of them and their miserable tool was the idea of union, not the idea they had thought of, but the Messianic idea. Seen from above, the individual folly of men served reason, which rules time and will some time fulfill it" (439). Feucht-wanger sees himself standing above the historical situation of his day and speaking in a timeless context.[51] This self-decep-tion, however, amounts to an apologia of Hitler's regime, for Feuchtwanger makes the regime of Terence-Nero, and thus of Hitler, a historical necessity,[52] which advocates resignation rather than resistance. Such an attitude could comfort those Germans fortunate to escape the brutality of the Nazis, but is an undelivered message of despair for others less fortunate. Though the latter was surely not intended, the discrepancy between Feuchtwanger's genuine and positive intentions and their actual expression in this parody contributes in large mea-sure to the overall literary weakness of the novel. Feucht-wanger, in effect, fails to manipulate Clio in the service of Calliope; instead, author, Calliope, and Clio work at cross-purposes throughout.

Heinrich Mann
Henri Quatre

Heinrich Mann's two-volume *Henri Quatre*[53] is neither a recon-struction of history for its own sake nor the mere transposition of contemporary figures and events into a historical setting. It is instead a parable showing that evil can be overcome by fighters who have learned to think and by thinkers who have learned to fight.[54] Henri Quatre becomes the symbol of man's struggle for self-knowledge, the embodiment of civilizing values, the representative of good, the union of intellect and power, the conqueror of evil and superstition, the expression of activist humanism.[55] This symbolic significance, however, is distilled through the portrayal of Henri as a man of the people and as king, for he is at one and the same time a natural creature of instinct and a man of reason, the common man and the exemplary hero.[56]

Young Henry of Navarre traces the development of Henri from the innocence of childhood through the apprenticeship of life to the threshold of the throne. His apprenticeship is a perpetual cycle of civil war, imprisonment and liberation, victory and defeat, hope and despair. Henri, a Huguenot of princely blood, learns the dangers of life, suffers the suppression of thought and religion, narrowly escapes the massacre of St. Bartholomew, and is schooled in the arts of disguise and treachery to become the focal point in the fight against the decadence of the House of Valois and the power-hungry machinations of the Guises and the Catholic League. He becomes the leader of the people because he acts on their behalf rather than on his own. Henry, King of France marks the end of Henri's youth and follows his path to the throne of France, through the turbulent years in power, to his death. His greatest mission is to establish a rule of tolerance, decency, and peace, initially for France and later for Europe. To this end he issues the Edict of Nantes and formulates his Great Plan. He must learn the relativity of all things, however, even of good, and the limitations of his power. He must also recognize his own imperfection and that of mankind. Henri, a prince of peace and the arbiter of Europe, dies a victim of political fanaticism. His death, however, is his final victory, for the people recognize in his death the significance of his life, a significance which lives beyond the grave.

Both the span of Henri's life, covered in the two volumes from childhood to victory over death, and the tension between Henri the man/king and Henri the immortal symbol are reflected in the first few paragraphs of volume I.[57] In this sense, the title of the first chapter, "The Beginning," is, by way of contrast, future-oriented. The very first sentence, "The boy was small and the mountains were enormous" (I, 3), places Henri immediately within nature, as one of its creatures. In addition, it is a statement of one against many. The mountains not only represent natural barriers and obstructions, but symbolize as well the immense obstacles to be overcome by Henri within his own nature, the obstacles strewn on the path which leads to the throne of France, and the obstacles he encounters in pursuing his mission.

The paths that Henri takes as a child in nature, a child of nature, and a child of France are narrow and dangerous. Just as he surveys the forested mountains with the sharp eyes of youth, he learns in the apprenticeship of life and his rule as king to "see," not only himself but the chaotic world around him. It is this self-knowledge and knowledge of others that allow him to traverse these paths.

Henri's close association with the people is also shown in this first chapter, but the fact that he is, by virtue of his royalty, above and apart from the people also indicates the relationship which determines the course of his life. The portrayal of Henri baking bread and drinking wine with the people is symbolic of his natural communion with them, but these same elements take on added significance when contrasted with the word "mass" which "had so terrible an effect that brother was no longer understood of brother, and became of alien blood" (I, 6). Attention is immediately focused on the constellation of religious war, in which religion plays no role.

Of equal importance in this first chapter is the scene involving Henri and the little girl. His instinctual sex drive—which will play a central role in his life—is already present on the subconscious level of this four-year-old.[58] This simple scene of youthful innocence, love, and determination embodies his attitude towards France; while all of Henri's loves and emotional attachments to women are genuine relationships of Henri the man, they also represent the symbolic relationship between Henri and France, for "it was woman that bound him to his people. In her he knew them, in her he made them his; and he was grateful" (I, 422). Henri's life is virtually a continuous love affair with France. Looking at the procession of women and lovers who play a role in his life, it becomes clear that they invariably reflect the immediate relationship between Henri and France. Jeanne, Katherine, Margot, Fleurette, and Corisande represent the most diverse elements in the course of Henri's ascent to the throne: Huguenot heritage, connection to the House of Valois, confrontation with Catholicism and the Guises, civil war, communion with the people, and growing support from the people. His love affair with Gabrielle, the object of his longest-enduring and most significant affections, parallels and reflects his years of rule. His relationships with Maria, Henriette, and Charlotte reflect the successive stages in the decline of his power as king.

Just as Henri challenges the larger youth and carries the little girl across the stream, he challenges France's warring factions, prevents the country from falling into the hands of the Guises, and carries it into a new era, instinctively sure of himself and the steps he takes despite recurrent scepticism. "Aut vincere aut mori," meaningless to the four-year-old, becomes the true motto for Henri's life, through which the saying gains extended meaning, for he does conquer: he is victor, even over death.

The major characters as well as the structure of the novel focus on the central figure and symbol of Henri. The characters, for instance, represent either stages in Henri's development, influences on his character, or aspects of his personality. In volume I this is especially reflected in the figures of Mornay, Du Bartas, D'Aubigné, and Montaigne.[59]

Mornay, the fanatic moral puritan who preaches the domination of the spirit over the flesh, is almost the exact opposite of Henri. This very extremism, however, attracts Henri, for his own conscience is in many respects embodied by Mornay. Du Bartas represents the Huguenot readiness for self-sacrifice, the strength behind Henri's cause. He, in contrast to Henri, is convinced that the world is incapable of redemption and therefore seeks death in battle for the cause rather than its attainment. D'Aubigné represents youthful innocence, impulsiveness, and enthusiasm, all of which are a part of Henri. This side of Henri is portrayed with clarity in the chapter "A Voice" (I, 287–90), in which he hears his other self speaking through the mouth of D'Aubigné.

Most important in Henri's development is his encounter with Montaigne,[60] which marks the beginning of the process of his self-knowledge. Montaigne has a clarifying and liberating effect on Henri. He teaches him to recognize certain principles in life, principles which Henri intuitively wishes to follow but which have not yet been consciously formulated within him. Montaigne familiarizes him with the formulation of scepticism— "How do I know?" (I, 305)—and the Ciceronian precept—"nihil est tam populare quam bonitas" (I, 306)—offering the possibility of scepticism and goodness as an intellectual approach to oneself and the world.

Montaigne expresses what Henri had feared to think: that nothing is further from religion than religious wars. Montaigne's "How do I know?" in answer to Henri's question about the true religion means repudiating Jeanne and Coligny, who fervently believed in their cause and whom Henri had honored as his moral guides. But Montaigne teaches him moderation in all things, even goodness, for excessive zeal turns any right into wrong (I, 404–05). The fanaticism of Jeanne and Mornay is just as dangerous as that of the Valois, the Guises, and the League.

The influence of Montaigne leads Henri to the inner consciousness of action. Henri's strength lies in his closeness to and knowledge of the people, in whom the moral qualities of tolerance and humanity are inherent, even though inactive. The humanist must act, however, in order to realize his goals and must not shy away from force if necessary: "A man must have this knowledge; he who thinks, and only he, must act. On the other side stands the moral horror beyond the confines of reason; the deeds of ignorant men, of men violent through excess of folly. Their temptation and their opportunity is force. Behold the kingdom! Left to itself, it will become a morass of blood and deceit, and no upstanding, wholesome race could grow to fullness on such soil, if we humanists cannot also ride and fight. Aha! Be very sure that we shall ride and fight!" (I, 488–89).

The moral certainty of Mornay, the idealism of Du Bartas, the innocence and militant humanism of D'Aubigné, and the wisdom of Montaigne are united in the person of Henri in volume I. In volume II the two most important figures are Rosny and Gabrielle, for they represent opposing natures within Henri. Rosny is the inscrutable pragmatist, the calculating diplomat, the executor of the possible, unhampered by emotion in arriving at necessary courses of political action. Gabrielle, on the other hand, is the expression of human love and emotion. Since both natures are combined in his person and act as the source of his greatness and strength, Henri can reject neither, just as he is incapable of rejecting Rosny for Gabrielle or Gabrielle for Rosny (II, 461).

the narrator foretells the course of Henri's life in the beginning of volume II and draws a clear correlation between Henri's relationship to Gabrielle and his relationship to France, for the pronoun "she" could apply equally to both: "She now gave herself in friendly fashion, but no more; for she was frank and would not feign. But what she did not yet feel he would make her feel; he would strive and he would win her tenderness, her ardour, her ambition, her devoted loyalty. He always came upon a new discovery; upon each step of these relations he entered a new world. Indeed, as King and man he changed as often as she, through him, became another woman. He would belie and shame himself that she might love him; abjure his religion and win the kingdom. He would be a conqueror, the shield of the weak, the hope of Europe—he would grow great" (II, 113–14).

After Gabrielle's death, the Rosny aspect of Henri's character takes over but overextends itself. Henri gives Rosny absolute military power, conceives his Great Plan, and wages war for the sake of peace. All of these actions, undertaken in the spirit of human decency and world peace rather than self-aggrandizement and personal political conquest, fail in the end, for they represent goals beyond the limits of Henri's power.

Henri acknowledges his limitations and sees his work as incomplete but his mission as nevertheless accomplished. He compares himself to Elizabeth of England, for both " 'had needed to be strong and to exalt the office of King—but not by way of disparaging humanity. They should see and recognize their own earthly greatness symbolized in Majesty' " (II, 611). Henri had sensed from the beginning that the people would recognize themselves in him only after his death (II, 306). This is the immortality that he gains, his victory over death, the immortality of humanism in the face of fanaticism.

Just as these major characters focus on the central figure of Henri, the structure of the novel also centers on Henri.[61] The two volumes are organized into books which are subdivided into short chapters. The titles of the books mark stages of Henri's life, and the titles of the chapters offer a running commentary on the action of the novel. Each chapter presents an individual scene or episode which directly relates to the other chapters and which offers an individual phase or aspect of Henri's life. Each chapter also takes on symbolic significance that points to a unity beyond the plurality of the individual scenes. This is especially evident in the contrasting or coupling of chapters.[62] "The Maze," for example, shows Henri and Margot in their honesty, simplicity, and instinctive naturalness, surrounded by nature itself. This chapter is juxtaposed to "A Ballet of Welcome," however, which symbolically draws Henri into the real maze of the pomposity and decadence of the Louvre. Similarly, "The Royal Banquet," with the pomp and disguised hate at the court, is juxtaposed to "The Tavern," with the naturalness and openness of the common people.

In like manner, Mann constructs a triad such as "The Rumour"–"The Reality"–"A Fairy-Tale," which focuses on Henri's ascension to the throne from different perspectives and with different emphases. Other triads, such as "Greatness from Within"–"Greatness in Action"–"Visible Greatness" and "Gabrielle: Life and Death"–"Gabrielle: In the Balance"–"Gabrielle: Abandoned," channel certain currents of development into a restricted area so that the central theme of the triad can be viewed in its totality and the end of the development can be foreseen. Moreover, these two triads are juxtaposed to each other in order to illuminate the crisis enveloping Henri in his relationship to Gabrielle.

In volume I, each book ends with a moral in French, which represents thematically and stylistically a third level of expression. The titles of the books and chapters are key words or phrases that point to the action and development of the novel. The chapters themselves enlarge upon these words and phrases by way of the plot. The moral then distills this multiplicity and combines a summary of each phase of Henri's life with a commentary and critique of his actions.

In Volume II a moral does not appear at the end of each book; instead, an allocution is placed at the very end. This allocution serves much the same function as the morals. Rather than reflecting on a particular book or even on the second volume, however, it reflects on the totality of the novel and the significance of Henri as a parabolic figure.

Here the use of the French—regarded as the language of reason, clarity, and precision[63]—not only sets the morals and the allocution in sharp contrast to the German, but also imbues them with a quality of critical objectivity and distance. They therefore contrast the multiplicity, emotion, and chaos of life with the unity, reflection, and clarity of reason.

The allocution at the end of volume II clearly points to a major aspect of the relationship between the novel and Mann's contemporary world. Through Henri, Mann addresses his contemporaries to draw attention to Henri's significance: "Regardez-moi dans les yeux. Je suis un homme comme vous; la mort n'y fait rien, ni les siècles qui nous séparent. Vous vous croyez de grandes personnes, appartenant à une humanité de trois cents ans plus âgée que de mon vivant. Mais pour les morts, qu'ils soient morts depuis si longtemps ou seulement d'hier, la différence est minime. Sans compter que les vivants de ce soir sont les morts de demain" (II, 784).

In his portrayal of Henri Quatre, Mann celebrates and issues an urgent appeal on behalf of the civilizing values of humanity, values which are threatened in his own age by Fascism and Nazism. He presents Henri as a parabolic mirror, in which mankind should recognize these values in itself and fight anew for their implementation in the world. Mann holds up this mirror in the first instance to France, which he sees as the only European country capable of checking the threat of Fascism.[64] Henri's closing words are intended to reawaken the activist humanism which he represents: "Je ne suis pas mort. Je vis, moi, et ce n'est pas d'une manière surnaturelle. Vous me continuez" (II, 785).

As a symbol of humanistic and civilizing values, Henri is contrasted to Hitler and Nazism[65] as well as with the court of the Valois, the Guises, and the Catholic League. The House of Valois is decadent, the Guises are power-hungry opportunists, and the League is their organ for fanatical religious persecution. The cruelty and depravity of the Valois Court, the persecution of the Huguenots, and the massacre of St. Bartholomew contain unmistakable references to the Hitler regime, the persecution of

German Jews and intellectuals, and the Nazi concentration camps.

Exile is a theme that clearly connects the novel to Mann's contemporary world. Jeanne and Henri's flight from Paris to La Rochelle is one into exile, no less than was the flight from Germany to France for many Germans. Jeanne's words express the initial reaction of those exiles who found refuge from Nazi persecution: " 'How good it is to come out of the land of hate and persecution into a city of kindliness and safety!' " (I, 51). The most explicit reference to exile is exemplified in Mornay, who managed to make his way through the massacre of St. Bartholomew and reach England, "the land of emigrants" (I, 390), where he awaited peace. Just as England had become Mornay's refuge, so France became a refuge for German emigrants or exiles who had fled Nazi persecution.

Even the contrast of internalized and actual emigration is presented in the figures of Henri and Mornay. While Mornay succeeded in reaching England, Henri was forced to remain in the Louvre as Katherine's prisoner. Forced to become Catholic and cut off from his friends, he was unable to trust anyone. The exchange between Mornay and Henri later is revealing and prophetic: " 'We have had a good deal to learn, eh, Mornay? Yours was a sorry life in exile.' 'And yours, too, in the Louvre' " (I, 433).

The situation and the mentality of exiles in Mann's own day is emphasized in Mornay's recollection of his exile in England: "The fugitive Protestant's property had been confiscated, and if he had been caught in his own country he would have ended his life in prison or on the scaffold" (II, 141). His helplessness when confronted by England's disbelief regarding the massacre of St. Bartholomew directly parallels the problem in Mann's age of directing the world's attention to the threat and horrors of Nazism. The threat and horrors are so great and so far removed from the everyday life of the rest of the world that the exile begins to despair in the face of this disbelief: "Deeds so horrible, that cried aloud to God, should surely have roused the world: a hundred miles away, in another Christian realm, they were no more than a tale that is told, which might have been a better one" (II, 142).

Mann even touches upon the problems of language and the

difficulties in publishing that the exile encountered in a foreign country. Mornay tries to have his theological writings printed in London, but the publishers refuse, "afraid of certain views that were interdicted even in that Protestant land. Others insisted that the author must write in English, not in Latin" (II, 142).

In the allegorical picture of Christianity which Lord Burghley's son sketches, Mann points to the political situation of twentieth-century Europe. The sketch shows an edifice supported by a row of pillars, representing the countries of Europe. A demon sets fire to one pillar, the fire spreads, a Christian bystander laments the situation but does nothing to stop it. The edifice, however, does not fall. Mornay calls this "The Mystery of Injustice" (II, 141). This is, in effect, Mann's profession of optimism in the face of catastrophe: the demon of fanaticism against Christianity then, Hitler and Nazism against human values now. The pillars in both cases, the countries of Europe, may be destroyed, but the edifice somehow survives. In connection with this sketch and "The Mystery of Injustice," Mann reaches into the farthest recesses of the psychology of the exile. Through Mornay he portrays the secret enhancement of the self which the exile feels by virtue of being persecuted (II, 143).

Additional points of reference to Mann's contemporary world are presented through other figures. Pastor Boucher, Henri Guise, and the Catholic League show the most direct references to Goebbels, Hitler, and the Nazis. Boucher is characterized at the founding of the League as "a preacher of a new fashion. At his very first words he foamed at the lips, and his rasping voice rose into an almost feminine shriek" (I, 344). He warns his captive audience that "the people and all that they stood for were in bitter peril, delivered up to secret forces which had sworn their overthrow" (I, 346), but assures them "that God had sent them a leader" (I, 347), Henri Guise. The ease with which Guise assumes the role of leader lies in the character of the people and his manner of seducing the masses. By subjugating themselves to him completely, they relinquish all personal responsibility (I, 350). Their pliability had already been noted by Henri after the massacre of St. Bartholomew: "'How easily they were persuaded into villainy and brutishness. . . . Burghers and mob combined form, when occasion favours, a rabble'" (I, 255).

The absurdity of Hitler's attempt to legitimize himself as the heir to the Holy Roman Empire of the German Nation is counterpointed in Henri's outburst over the claim of Guise: " 'That ruffian Guise! Now he claims descent from Charlemagne. . . . A low-born imposter from across the frontier dares to call us bastards, and himself heir to the crown of France' " (I, 514–15).

These points of comparison are obvious but never forced. Guise, Boucher, and the League are not equated with Hitler, Goebbels, and the Nazi Party; they remain episodic, satirical, and grotesque, even as reflected images of the contemporary world.[66] Although Mann utilizes history as a parable to illuminate the present, this, in turn, illuminates the past, for Mann consciously obliterates any demarcation between the two: "Cette époque m'a fait faire toutes sortes de découvertes morales. . . . (En disant *cette époque* je confonds les deux, celle où je suis et celle que je pense. A la longue elles ne font qu'une)."[67] Mann sees the events of the twentieth century, in regard to European unity and nationalism, as a process which spans the sixteenth and twentieth centuries.[68] Heinrich Mann thus transforms the historical figure of Henri Quatre into a parable for his contemporary world in order to show this process within its total context.

Alfred Döblin
Amazonas

Alfred Döblin's *Amazonas* trilogy[69] reveals a visible metamorphosis in its development.[70] It begins as a hymnal celebration of primal nature, with a major interest in the historical material itself. In the course of working with the material, however, Döblin is confronted with the rise of Nazism and the phenomenon of exile, both of which he begins to see in relation to his material, resulting in a modification of his concept of the historical novel and of the influence that Calliope should exert over Clio.[71] *Amazonas* thus transcends the original material to become symbolic, exemplary, and parabolic, a historical novel which bears indirect as well as direct reference to Döblin's contemporary world.[72]

Seen as a totality, the trilogy is not directly concerned with the primitive religions and societies of nature of the South American Indians; the conquest of these Indians by barbaric European white men; the founding, growth, and destruction of the Jesuits' Christian republic in Paraguay; the court and papal intrigues in Europe in the sixteenth and seventeenth centuries; or the loosely connected fates of certain individuals of the twentieth century. Instead, these elements illuminate the existential dilemma of man, expressed as a consequence of alienation and the social structures within which man is supposed to find guidelines for existence and thus meaning in life. *Amazonas* is therefore connected to Döblin's previous works in a transitional capacity. Rather than a definitive break with past views, the trilogy represents an evolutionary reappraisal of those views.[73] Döblin perceives man as part of an animated, ordered, dynamic, finite, and infinite nature—man as the finite, ephemeral form in the infinite process of cyclical rejuvenation. The possibility of living in harmony with such a nature, open to the primitive jungle tribes of South America through viable mythical-mystical relationships, is no longer available to modern man, who is totally alienated from nature.

Man's endeavors, however, are directed towards re-establishing basic relationships—man to man, man to nature, man to society—in order to give life meaning. These endeavors usually become vain attempts to rediscover Eden, seeking happiness and meaning outside the self, but in this world. Such attempts are doomed to fail, because rational man tries to attain this goal by subduing nature and his environment rather than by finding a mythical-mystical basis for his existence. In the last analysis, human love provides such a basis and the goal becomes not one of success but one of endeavor.[74] It is in striving for human love that the harmony between man and man, man and nature, man and society, and man and the universe can perhaps be re-established.

It is not merely a question of the individual's assuming a passive or an active attitude in coming to terms with the existential dilemma, but rather a question of the total context within which such a dilemma develops. These are the aspects of man's existence expressed in Döblin's trilogy, ranging from the primitive jungle societies of the Indians in South America to the technological world of the twentieth century.

The title of the trilogy as well as the titles of the individual volumes express the major aspects of the trilogy in symbolic images. "Amazonas," the title originally intended for the entire trilogy, alludes to the seasonal flooding of the Amazon, which destroys jungle life but brings forth new life. It is, as such, amoral, expressing the nature of the infinite primal force of both jungle and human existence. This force witnesses repeated cycles as they arise from and pass again into the anonymous flow of existence, demonstrated in the trilogy by successive waves of Indian tribes, white conquistadors and settlers, the Jesuits—and by extension the parties to the Thirty Years' War—the Humanists, and the technological man of the twentieth century. It is this primal force pronouncing its infinite nature over the finite nature of a human cycle of existence that is contained in the cry of the Amazon: "You were never here!" (82).

The titles of the three volumes outline the course of a single cycle within the infinite nature of the Amazon. "The Land Without Death" symbolizes the state of man after emergence from the anonymous flow of existence, in which he seeks resonance with its primal force. On the level of the organic jungle tribe, this is possible, for the harmony between man and the elemental forces of nature has not been destroyed. Rational man, however, is alienated from nature. He recognizes harmony in nature but not in his own existence, which he finds wretched and meaningless. He seeks to regain this harmony by force of action, but his search and mode of action are misdirected. Since man wants to find harmony in the cycle of his own existence, he seeks an earthly paradise, and, to attain it, directs his action against nature and the very harmony he seeks. Thus, the search for the Land Without Death represents a vain search and brings the concept of human action into question.

"The Blue Tiger" symbolizes the destructive force which enters the cycle when man's search for the Land Without Death comes to represent the misuse of the insights into the nature of his existence that man has gained. This corresponds to the flooding aspect of the Amazon, but, unlike the amoral aspect of the river, the appearance of the Blue Tiger represents the destructive force of evil in man.

"The New Jungle" symbolizes the completion of the cycle. Each attempt to find the Land Without Death, which ends in the advent of the Blue Tiger, sends one cycle of human existence back into the anonymous flow but allows another cycle to begin. Thus, the progression that leads from the natural jungle of primitive South American Indians to the new technological jungle of twentieth-century man is a progression of the cycles expressed in the three titles of the volumes, all of which occur in the infinite flow of the "Amazonas" concept of existence.

The three volumes also represent three distinct stages in the development of man: the primal order of the jungle in volume I, the religious order of Christianity in volume II, and the rational order of the modern technological world in volume III. Though elements of all three are present in each volume, one order dominates. In each volume, there are those who succeed and those who fail in establishing a mythical-mystical relationship in order to overcome the self-alienating nature of man: the organic jungle tribes as opposed to the Inca State and the Amazon tribes; the Jesuit Republic, in its original intent, as opposed to a Europe of the Inquisition and the Thirty Years' War; and Klinkert as opposed to Jagna and Theresa.

Since the historical material serves a symbolic function, it becomes significant only as it relates to the question of modern man's existence. But the tendency to contrast the jungle and the Indians of South America with the white men of Europe and their world, and then to draw a connection to twentieth-century man, is all too tempting and just as misleading. The differences here, which can be mistakenly interpreted as intentional contrasts, are not differences of kind but of degree and manifestation. The real nature of the trilogy demands an investigation of correspondences and parallels rather than of contrasts.[75]

The significance of such an approach is immediately clear in regard to the collision of two opposing worlds—those of the Indians and the conquistadors. The conquistadors do not actually introduce any elements, which, in one form or another, are not already present in South America. The actual collision is not between races or peoples, but between two types of nature: primal nature as expressed in the jungle, and the artificial nature of a man-made environment. This collision, however, occurs in South America among the Indians before the arrival of the white man. The Inca State in opposition to the organic jungle tribe is but one example, significant because it symbolizes nothing less than the irreconcilable polarities within man himself: born of nature but opposed to it, passive but yet active.[76]

Another point of comparison is the search for the Land Without Death. Coincidental with the arrival of the white men in South America, two tribes of Indians, the Toad People and the Duck People, set out to find the Land Without Death. That is exactly what the conquistadors themselves unconsciously hope to find. The only difference in their vain search for this utopia is that, whereas the Indians actually believe in its palpable existence, the white men, taught by Christianity, believe that paradise is the province of the hereafter. The character of the Indian as well as of the white man is thus split, and both are alienated from nature: the one from the primal jungle, the other from an artificial nature, which in turn is already alienated from primal nature through the teachings of Christianity.

The case of the conquistadors resembles that of twentieth-century man. Whereas Christianity had lost its role as the defining force of existence for the conquistadors, technology and science are incapable of defining the force of existence for Jagna, Theresa, and Klinkert. Like the Indians and the conquistadors, they too set out to find the Land Without Death in their own fashion.

Interwoven into this search is the motif of cruelty which is tied to the social structure. It is irrelevant that certain innocent acts by the Indians contrast with certain barbaric acts by the white men. What is important is not how the Indians regard the actions of the white men and vice versa, but how the Indians and the white men regard their own actions. Despite their cultic-mythical context, the actions of the Indians are by no means idealized or made palatable.[77] The sacrifice of children, the Amazons' murder of their mates after the wedding night, the Indians' murder of Las Casas can all be explained and understood in the context out of which they arise, but they remain, nevertheless, acts of cruelty. The important point is that they are not committed merely for the sake of cruelty but have meaning for those who perform them, and, in their primal forms, for those against whom the acts are directed. They fit into the natural order of the Indians' existence.

The process of alienation from this natural order is already in evidence among the Indians of South America, however, especially in the highly developed political state of the Incas and in the tribes of the Amazons. Acts of cruelty take on a different dimension in the Inca State, because the state is an artificial power structure devoid of the primal relationship between man and nature. The state attempts to create its own cultic-mythical context of existence, but that context is hollow. The actions of the state are wholly impersonal. Acts of cruelty in the tribes of the Amazons develop from an existential necessity to cruelty for its own sake. In both cases, the actions lose real meaning in a cultic–mythical context of existence and carry with them the seeds of destruction.

This degeneration of context is the primary point of comparison for the white men, ranging from the conquistadors to Jagna, Theresa, and Klinkert. Christianity, although it contributed to man's alienation from primal nature, was able to define and provide meaning for man's existence as long as it was an organic structure which expressed the relationships between man and existence in a cultic-mythical context. The Church, however, alienated Christianity from itself when it misused this context and became an artificial, worldly power structure, comparable to the Inca State. With the advent of the Reformation and Humanism, which can be seen as attempts to re-establish such a context for Christianity, and, for the first time, a rational-scientific context for existence, the viability of the Church was destroyed, but not the Church itself. Instead, it became a self-destructive force, exemplified in the Inquisition and the Thirty Years' War.[78] With the meaning of existence destroyed, the white men fled to the jungles of South America, seeking the Land Without Death or—in its stead—death itself.

The Jesuits, who are aware of this alienation of the Church from Christianity, hope to re-establish a Christian mythical-mystical basis of existence in the jungles of South America. They are confronted, however, by the natural mythical-mystical basis of existence already evident among the Indians. The Jesuits do not actually succeed in Christianizing the Indians, for the Indians absorb Christianity into their religion of nature and hope that the Jesuits will establish an earthly paradise for them. Actually it is the Jesuits who come to believe in the Land Without Death and who try to create the Land of Canaan anew. Thus their failure to influence the Indians is revealed in the fact that they are destroyed both when they remain passive and when they become active by establishing an artificial state which is, in effect, alienated from their original Christian mission.[79]

Modern rationalism and science, outgrowths of Humanism, hoped to re-establish the relationship between man and nature on a different plane. It was rationalism, however, that produced man's awareness of the irreconcilable conflict in his own existence. The growth of science only widened the gap between the two poles, as man became aware of his power as creator within nature. Science and technology became the religions that replaced Christianity in the twentieth century, but because they disallow the cultic-mythical context for existence—the only manner in which the gap between the two irreconcilable poles can be bridged—they succeeded only in alienating man from his artificial environment. This is the situation in which Jagna, Theresa, and Klinkert find themselves. They, like the conquistadors, can find no meaning in existence and seek the Land Without Death or death in their own manner.

Jagna, Theresa, and Klinkert have no meaningful relationship to society, nature, or religion. Reality is defined in terms of technology and science, but these fail to provide a meaning for their existence. In their search for such a meaning, all are transformed in some manner. Jagna and Theresa find death, he in the jungles of South America, she in suicide. Ironically, these deaths have meaning only insofar as they release Jagna and Theresa from an otherwise meaningless existence. Klinkert, on the other hand, is able to find a personal meaning in life through love. The conflicts they face, their actions and their fates, are not unlike those of the Indians, the conquistadors, and the Jesuits. All are confronted by the active-passive voice which contradicts itself: "Give up, there is no salvation. . . . Keep going, do not yield, ever!" (NJ, 390).

The guiding principle in Jagna's life is women. As his awareness of their meaninglessness for him increases, so does Jagna's awareness of his capability of and pleasure in cruelty. Self-hate and a feeling of impotence within society develop out of his existential dilemma. Since his society holds no meaning for him, he finds no reason to seek a meaning in life. He opposes his environment by emigrating to South America, but this action is also meaningless, for he passively succumbs to the forces of nature, proving that modern man cannot return to nature on the level of the primitive jungle tribes.[80]

Theresa is the counterpart to Jagna. She attempts to act within society by collecting men, but her action is directed towards self-destruction. She seeks a man who can destroy her and thus release her from an existence devoid of meaning.

The guiding principle in Klinkert's life is action based on situational ethics. Technology connected with logical consequentiality are his guidelines. Power, force, and unlimited authority are his goals. In effect, this is the supporting philosophy of National Socialism. Through his experience with Theresa and his genuine love for Maria—the religious implications of which are clear—he comes to realize that man is more than an object, a number, or a machine.[81] Although he has found personal meaning in life, he is unable to act. Thus, he opposes his environment passively through inner emigration.

Posten, who holds the same initial views as Klinkert, is the only figure who remains unchanged, the pragmatist who adapts to every situation. He subordinates his individuality, and with it his individual responsibility, to his environment—the artificial, technological state. Although he inwardly opposes the rise of National Socialism, he adapts himself to it, rationalizing it as a passing phenomenon.

These figures are presented to Galileo, Copernicus, and Giordano Bruno to demonstrate the wretched state of modern man and to assign blame to science for the destruction of man's existential base and the failure to provide a substitute. While Galileo and Copernicus accept the blame, Bruno adamantly refuses to do so. Bruno is shocked by the state of modern man, but he confesses only to having made man a creator, not to being responsible for his present state. He firmly believes that suffering induces man to reflect upon his existence, and that love reveals the most profound basis of truth (NJ, 493). Therefore, the sufferings of Jagna, Theresa, and Klinkert do have meaning if they serve as a basis for greater insight into their lives. Bruno also realizes that the existential problem of man is ultimately without solution. The elements of alienation in man will always exist as well as the active-passive nature in man which tries to overcome this alienation. The recognition of this fact is contained in Bruno's paradoxical outcry: " 'Oh, defiled world! Oh, magnificent Earth!' " (NJ, 496).

Bruno's admonition that he was called upon five hundred years too soon, for the world is "im Fluss" (both in flux and in the river), becomes an expression with multi-level meaning, for the world, i.e., the meaning of existence, is expressed symbolically in the river and its spirit, Sukuruja. Until man has grasped the symbolic significance of the Amazon and Sukuruja, man will remain locked in an existential dilemma. Jagna, Theresa, and Klinkert are but finite cycles within the infinite course of existence, and as such are no different than the Indians, the conquistadors, and the Jesuits. The overwhelming aspect of environment or nature applies to all of the figures in the trilogy, whether they gain insight or not. Klinkert is able to find truth in love, but his environment is so overwhelming that he is unable to apply his own insight to his collective society. The unsuccessful Jesuit experiment is the only attempt to apply gained insight actively to a collective society.

Despite the ultimate failure of such attempts, Bruno acknowledges the many cycles that will come, each with the possibility of bringing forth new forms. The inherent hope is that some day forms will emerge which are in closer harmony with their environment, a harmony comparable to that of the primitive organic jungle tribes of South America, although on a different plane. This optimism, faced with the portent of National Socialism, is supported by Döblin: "Patience, patience was the important word. Time, stronger than bloodhounds and weapons, became a force which could not be taken from man" (NJ, 517).

These major themes and points of comparison are supported by a vast number of lesser, but nevertheless significant, parallels. These also point out that the essence of the trilogy lies in comparison and parallelism rather than in contrast, for these parallels reveal stark similarities of action and response within each of the three major stages in the development of man as represented in the three volumes: primal nature, Christianity, and the technological world of the twentieth century.[82]

The Indian's relationship to his totem parallels the European's relationship to God and the initial relationship between modern man and scientific technology. The Indians believe that they descend from their totem just as Christians believe they are creations of God and modern man believes in the omnipotence of science. As long as the totem, or its equivalent in Christianity or science, is honored in a mythical-mystical relationship to existence, man lives in harmony with his environment, be it primal jungle nature or man-made. When the relationship to the totem is destroyed, chaos follows, for the base of existence crumbles. The arrival of white men in South America only intensifies the process of destruction which is already present, just as the advent of Humanism and science only intensifies the process of destruction which is already present in the Church. Christianity ultimately fails to replace natural religion in South America, just as science ultimately fails to replace Christianity in Europe.

Another parallel is evidenced in the actions of Toeza and Bruno. Both break with existing structures of existence, both witness the results of their actions, and both are powerless to change or affect the course of their actions. Toeza recognized the servile position of woman in a patriarchal society. She wanted to liberate woman by breaking with the traditional order and founding an Amazon State. She witnesses the cruel excesses of her descendants, especially those of Truvanare, and sees that her action has led to evil. She despairs and does not intervene in the destruction of the Amazon State—the appearance of the Blue Tiger—because this would only perpetuate the evil which has arisen. Bruno's action in proposing natural science theories in opposition to the Church is a similar break with traditional structures of existence. He too witnesses the approach of the Blue Tiger in the form of National Socialism; he too must acknowledge the cruelty that has arisen from his actions; he too does not intervene. Unlike Toeza, however, he does not despair. The difference in their attitudes lies in the qualitative difference in their actions. Toeza did not actually create anything new when she broke with the traditional order, for the state she creates is just as tyrannical as the one she wished to replace. In terms of the trilogy's symbolism, she did not succeed in bringing forth a new form within her finite cycle of existence. Bruno, on the other hand, did create something new by founding a new age, even though it became just as tyrannical a force as the Church he opposed. In both cases, however, the destruction that arises results from the inability of man to seize the opportunity for creating something new and integrating those aims into his environment.

There is also a parallel between the actions of Toeza and those of the Jesuits. Both represent attempts to unite diametrically opposed natures. The union of man and animal is not forbidden in the cultic-mythical order of the Indians, but neither is it condoned. Since the animal is perceived as stronger than man, such a union could produce a demonic hybrid. Toeza dares to enter into such a union by taking the jaguar, Walyarina, as her bridegroom. The results are the poisoning of the men in her tribe, the founding of the Amazon State, and discord between the tribes of men and the tribes of women. The Jesuits attempt a similar union between Christianity and the Indians' religion of nature, elements which are diametrically opposed. In the Christian view, man rules over nature; in the Indians' view, man is subservient to nature. This attempted union results in the figurative poisoning of relationships with other members of the Christian community in South America, the founding of the Jesuit Republic, and discord among the European "tribes." In both cases, the ultimate result is destruction.

A parallel exists, too, between the Inca State and the advent of National Socialism in the technological world of the twentieth century. Both represent totalitarian states which reduce man to the level of an object. Both of these forms of forced passivity, which is opposed to individuality and self-determination, negate or ignore the dual active-passive nature of man, and thus carry the seeds of destruction in them. Cuzumarra's relationship to the Inca State is similar to that of Klinkert's to his own world. Both believed in power and authority, both came to realize the meaninglessness of this order, both search for the meaning of existence. Both find it and both remain passive, unable to act. The inner conflict of Cuzumarra is resolved in death, that of Klinkert in love and inner emigration.

The central theme of the trilogy and the specific points of comparison have universal significance and are therefore broadly related to Döblin's contemporary world. In addition to this universality, however, certain elements of content and theme offer direct parallels to Döblin's contemporary world. The theme of actual and inner emigration, in regard to the actions of Jagna and Klinkert, has already been dealt with indirectly. More important, however, are the elements concerning the Jews and the figure of Hitler.

Döblin was active in the League for Jewish Colonization, but he saw the importance of the movement not so much in the acquisition of land and the physical settling of Jews as in a general intellectual and spiritual rejuvenation of Judaism, which should offer an alternative to the materialism of the Western World.[83] He had believed that the technological impulses of the natural sciences would promote the spiritual mastery of nature and eventually lead to a spiritual transcendence of nature. He was disappointed to discover that the task was too great, that the Jewish people were incapable of executing such a spiritual rejuvenation of mankind. His original beliefs in such a rejuvenation, however, are reflected in the attempts of the Jesuits to subjugate nature morally and to establish a truly Christian society.[84] The destruction of the Jesuit Republic and the advent of National Socialism reflect the collapse of Döblin's belief in this endeavor. Nevertheless, Döblin still portrays the original intent of the Jesuits and the attitude of Bruno in a positive light.

The figure of Hitler, his regime, and his treatment of the Jews are reflected in the last two chapters of volume II, "Pombal" and "The Last Jesuits." Pombal assumes control over a weak king on the throne of Portugal and finds the country in a wretched state. In dictatorial fashion, he begins to remedy this condition, but "with imprisonment, secret police, ax and exile, he drove justice out of the land" (621). He builds up a huge army and awaits a chance to act, which he finds in a minor incident involving an attack on the king. From this he fabricates a charge of massive conspiracy in order to destroy the power of the aristocracy, gain control of the courts, and persecute the Jesuits, who are branded as communists and made responsible for the miseries of Portugal. The persecution and execution of the Jesuit, Gabriel Malagrada, and the imprisonment of all Jesuits parallel the persecution of the Jews in Germany.

Döblin has utilized historical material in *Amazonas* to give literary expression to themes of universal as well as specific contemporary import. Volumes I and II are the illustrative, exemplary, and symbolic foundation out of which volume III grows. Aside from the overwhelming thematic ties that connect volumes I and II to volume III, the totality of the trilogy can only be understood from the perspective of volume III.[85] If one misses this basic relationship between the historical material and the actual literary content of the trilogy, which is itself a literary entity, one fails to understand the trilogy on its most basic level.[86]

Joseph Roth
The Ballad of the Hundred Days

Joseph Roth's *The Ballad of the Hundred Days*[87] exemplifies the subjective use of historical material to present two contemporary but universal themes: man's endeavor to give life meaning within an atmosphere of existential isolation, and the phenomenon of myth, a force related to but independent of the person with whom it is identified.[88] Both themes run parallel in their development and are intricately interwoven into and supported by the structure of the novel.[89] The work is divided into four books, two focused on the figure of Napoleon and two focused on the figure of Angelina, indicating that both figures play an equally important role in the development of these two interrelated themes.[90]

Both Napoleon and Angelina have abrogated the sense of belonging to a community of man by subjugating their lives to the Napoleon myth. Their isolation is identified with disintegration and disillusionment and is symbolized in the Marseillaise, which accompanies Napoleon and Angelina on their separate paths, Napoleon's into exile, Angelina's into death:

"To sing it in company with many others was to feel one's own loneliness in spite of the crowd. For the Marseillaise proclaimed both triumph and downfall, community with the world and the solitude of the spirit, the illusory power of man and his certain impotence. In it life and death were turned to song. It was the song of the people of France" (11).

The realization that life had been defined in terms of an impotent myth devoid of reality characterize the collapse of the Austrian Monarchy, which Roth experienced personally.[91] In the novel, Napoleon and Angelina are forced to come to terms with the collapse of the Napoleonic myth, which had served as the primary existential determinant for both. As it is gradually destroyed, they become ever more isolated. One solution to this problem is to establish a new determinant which can be correlated to reality. If this proves to be impossible, the only alternative solution is death.[92] By penetrating and rejecting his own myth and redefining his life in terms of God, Napoleon succeeds in finding a new determinant. Death, on the other hand, is the only solution for Angelina who is incapable of bridging the irreparable gap between the destroyed myth and reality.

The structure of the novel emphasizes this existential isolation: The few instances in which one figure plays a direct role in the books of the other only emphasize this total isolation, and the individual isolation of each is clearly presented within their own books. Napoleon, lacking both feeling for the community of man and any personal devotion, seeks fulfillment where it cannot be found—in power politics and war.[93] These endeavors only dissociate him more, for he comes to be regarded as the myth rather than the man. Angelina, too, is incapable of genuine personal devotion, and her attempts to overcome her isolation are powerless against the overwhelming influence of the myth.

The process by which Napoleon frees himself from his myth and finds the path to God is a gradual one full of ambivalence,[94] for he wavers between alienation from and identification with his myth. The white hands that reach out for him as he enters Paris, "hands such as are raised to the gods" (16), frighten and alienate him, but a few moments later in the privacy of his own quarters, he identifies with his myth: "He . . . smiled at his reflection, the great Emperor smiling at the great Emperor. He was pleased with himself" (21). This ambivalence is also present in Napoleon's relationship to God. Even though he acknowledges the existence of God in the beginning, the aura of the Napoleon myth overshadows any existential significance God could have for his own life. Nevertheless, he senses the underlying power of true belief and wavers between the two poles.

Waterloo, where Napoleon experiences a type of purgatory, marks a major turning point in the transition from the myth to the seeker of God. Before Waterloo, Napoleon had merely sensed the alienation between himself and the myth, himself and the masses, but now he clearly separates the two. Even though he has not yet rejected his myth, he has identified it as such. Here his isolation and despair are at their greatest, for he no longer has the myth as an existential anchor and has not yet found his way to God.

On his return to Paris, Napoleon is overpowered by the image of Job being humbled before God.[95] Whether or not the implied analogy between Napoleon and Job is legitimate is not important. However, what is important is that the rest of Napoleon's life through his surrender is characterized by the vacillation between this image of Job and the Napoleon myth. The myth of the worldly, powerful Napoleon is no longer tenable in view of his humbled position. Unable to reject the myth entirely, Napoleon contemplates himself: " 'I am more than an Emperor; I am an Emperor who is able to renounce. I had a sword in my hand and I let it fall. I sit on a throne and listen to the worms gnawing inside it. I sit on a throne and see myself lying in a coffin. I grasp a scepter and I wish to bear a cross. Yes, I wish to bear a cross! . . .' " (230). This mixture of humility and imperial arrogance marks the turning point toward transcending the limits of the old myth. In rejecting the worldly myth, however, he attempts to replace it with another. In self-delusion he removes his crown but sees the people of France placing an invisible crown on his head, making him the true Emperor, the true embodiment of the French people.[96]

Still struggling with this self-delusion, Napoleon tries to rationalize worldly power for the cause of Christ in a dream the night before his surrender, but the Holy Father in this vision has the final word: " 'The Church does not need emperors who are men of violence. You sent for me, I did not send for you! The Church is eternal, emperors are transitory' " (274). The dream embodies not only the historical circumstances of his coronation, but the vain attempts to rationalize his present fate. Napoleon thus loses another myth before it can materialize, but the pendulum of his behavior once again swings to the opposite extreme. In the scene before the mirror as he dresses for his surrender—antithetical to his behavior before this mirror in the beginning—Napoleon rejects the worldly myth so totally that he envisions himself an actor, playing the part of Napoleon the Emperor. Only as he goes to surrender, amid the final shouts of "Long live the Emperor" (278), does he begin to sense true humility and acknowledge the responsibility for his myth.

Napoleon's conversion is symbolized in the act of boarding the ship and sailing into exile, for he is entering a new realm.[97] The last image of Napoleon remains, however, that of a humbled man rather than of an entirely humble man, for his last utterance, the command " 'Open it!' " (283), is as ambivalent as the entire process of his conversion.

Whereas Napoleon's path led him from myth to God, Angelina's path leads in the opposite direction, moving from belief in God to become a meaningless sacrifice to the Napoleon myth. Although the irreversible process from God to myth has already set in when she first appears in the novel, her path is also gradual and ambivalent. Her existence as a simple washerwoman is initially defined equally by Church and Emperor. Her reverence for Napoleon's wet tracks in the imperial bath, her coveting the imperial handkerchief, and her vow to become beautiful for the Emperor as she bares her breast before the imperial mirror, however, represent an intricate combination of mythical and religious veneration, and eroticism. Although it is clear which determinant is the stronger, she still derives a portion of her existential determinant from the Church: "The cross brought her peace, but the handkerchief made her happy" (100). When Napoleon rejects her as a lover, however, she has nothing to fall back on but the waning power of the Church within her: "At night she scrambled through her prayers and gave the crucifix only a fleeting kiss. The Emperor's handkerchief lay hidden at the bottom of her wooden box" (107). Caught between the two extremes, she despairs, for the

Church, as an independent and genuine existential determinant, ceases to exist for Angelina, except in terms of the myth.

Symptomatic of Angelina's isolation is the series of love affairs with Sosthène Levadour, Charles Rouffic, and Jan Wokurka. These are attempts to fill the void left by the imperial rejection and are symbolic stages in the growing tension in the delicate thread that bridges the gap between myth and reality. The Napoleon myth gradually displaces the Church entirely and assumes a divine aura in addition to the erotic element. Angelina could have returned to Poland with Jan to begin a new life, but the power of the myth seizes her with greater strength than ever when Napoleon returns. Her prayers in the church are directed not to God but to the myth, and the immense distance between reality and myth is revealed in her belief that these prayers contributed to Napoleon's victory when, in fact, the victory celebration she hears marks Napoleon's decisive defeat at Waterloo. Since Angelina had defined her existence completely in terms of the myth, which has now collapsed, the delicate thread that held myth and reality together breaks. Trampled by royalists carrying an effigy of Napoleon, she is left to die on the street, believing that the rag effigy beside her is the real Emperor.

Stages in the parallel but opposing fates of Napoleon and Angelina are reflected in their brief encounters. Napoleon at first takes no notice of Angelina outside the imperial bath, but she is already caught up in the erotic form of the myth. Their second encounter, when Napoleon sees Angelina in his own quarters but rejects her as a lover, represents the climax and collapse of the erotic myth for Angelina. Although their meeting in the park provides Napoleon with some knowledge of her person, he soon forgets her. In stark contrast, Angelina kneels before him as before God. At their meeting following the death of Angelina's son, Napoleon reacts at last as a man, for he becomes aware of Angelina as an individual and as one who must suffer because of his myth. Angelina, however, remains a captive of the myth, and the grotesque encounter between her and the effigy of Napoleon symbolizes the opposing solutions to their fates.

Underlying the Napoleon myth as it relates to man's endeavor to give life meaning within an atmosphere of existential isolation is the phenomenon of the myth itself, expressed in a set of interrelationships: Napoleon (myth)–Napoleon (man); Napoleon (myth)–Angelina (the masses); and Napoleon (man)–Angelina (the masses). Although the novel is by no means a historical *roman à clef*, Roth's presentation of the myth phenomenon offers unmistakable reference to his contemporary world.[98]

Historically, the crisis of leadership in France prior to and throughout Napoleon's reign is very different from the crisis of leadership in Germany from the end of World War I through the dictatorship of Hitler. The need for a myth on the part of the people as well as on the part of the leader in such a time of crisis is, however, basic to both. In both instances a firm order to life is missing, and a myth arises out of pure existential need. The masses use such a myth to establish identity and secure their existence; the figurehead uses the myth to exercise power through the masses. It is totally irrelevant who the figurehead of the myth is, as long as the myth is maintained. In the novel, the French change figureheads like pairs of shoes, wavering between royalist and republican myths. The various factions may retain loyalty to one or the other, but the masses in general support the myth which happens to be present in France at the time, unaware that the real source of leadership is their own eagerness to be manipulated.

The portrayal of Napoleon and France at the beginning of the novel characterizes the bond created between the masses and the myth figure and points indirectly to the relationship between Hitler and the German masses as well as to any dictatorship in which the leader is surrounded by an aura of myth: "By exalting himself he ennobled, crowned, and exalted every individual member of the nameless herd, and that was why they loved him" (6). The consequences of this bond, supported by the need for the myth by the leader and the led, then becomes clear and offers direct implications for the psychology behind the fanaticism of Nazism: "He promised the people liberty and the integrity of the individual—but whoever entered his service rendered his freedom and became wholly subservient to him. . . . He did not trust men until they were ready to die for him—so he turned them into soldiers. In order that he might be sure of their affection, he taught them to obey him. In order that he might be sure of them, they had to die" (6–7). Even the erotic element in the relationship between Napoleon and Angelina reflects the psychology of Nazism in regard to the leader and the led, where death becomes the only union possible within the context of existential isolation and myth adoration.[99] Like Angelina, thousands of Germans were to die for a fanatical myth, oblivious to the grotesque reality of their existence.

Through the figure of Napoleon, Roth offers a counterfigure to the dictators of his own age.[100] Napoleon's conversion in the novel is genuine; he does not merely make virtue out of necessity.[101] Despite the similarities between Napoleon and Hitler in the beginning, one important difference remains: Napoleon gains insight into his myth, rejects it, and accepts the burden of responsibility for it. Roth does not dwell on or expand upon Napoleon's acceptance of this burden, for the myth is basically a creation of the masses and not of a single man, and the figurehead can only exploit that which is already present in the masses. Maintaining that Napoleon, or Hitler, bears sole responsibility for the acts committed in the name of the myth is too simplistic,[102] for it is not the man but the phenomenon which grasps the masses and leads to mass insanity. Roth's Napoleon recognizes this and rejects it; Hitler did neither.

The themes of existential isolation, the search for meaning in life, and the phenomenon of myth are interwoven into the structure of the novel to create an artistic whole. The choice of this particular material demands some degree of indebtedness to Clio, but it is clear that the historical material is not presented for its own sake. Roth calls upon Calliope in penetrating and transcending the material to produce a creative piece of historical fiction with both universal relevance and indirect reference to the real concerns of his own age.

Thomas Mann
The Beloved Returns

Thomas Mann's The Beloved Returns[103] is a historical novel in the sense that it utilizes historical material for a fictional presentation. Calliope manipulates Clio's contribution with a free hand, for the novel is not directly concerned with the person of Charlotte Kestner nor with the person of Goethe,[104] but rather with the phenomenon of the Werther experience, utilizing both Goethe and Charlotte Kestner as major examples. The historical material, the themes and ideas derived from it, the internal structure of the novel and the novel as a whole, the relationship between the author and the subject matter, and the relationship between the author's presentation of the subject matter and his contemporary world: all revolve around the central core of the Werther experience, which is essentially a process of spiritual and intellectual rebirth, a process in which the given realities of the past and present are synthesized and overcome in the present to provide greater insight into the future.

The structure of the novel offers insight into the interconnections of the various expressions of the Werther experience.[105] It is divided into nine chapters, each dominated by a particular perspective. The perspective in chapters one and two are represented by Mager and Rose Cuzzle, who have no direct relationship to Goethe but are merely attracted by the myth surrounding him. Riemer and Adele Schopenhauer, on the other hand, see the complexities and contradictions within the person of Goethe from their perspectives in chapters three and four. These four chapters, which alternate masculine with feminine perspectives, begin to close and focus on the person of Goethe in chapter five, in which the masculine and feminine aspects—an expression of totality in itself—are combined in Adele's tale concerning August and Ottilie, who have a closer relationship to Goethe and are influenced more directly by his genius. The focus in chapter five is broadened rather than sharpened, however, for the tale of August and Ottilie still remains the perspective of Adele. This broadened perspective is then sharpened in chapter six by August. Since August is merely an extension of Goethe's person, he has the closest connection to Goethe and is most strongly influenced by the phenomenon of Goethe. All of these perspectives, which nevertheless provide only limited insight into the phenomenon of the Werther experience, focus on Goethe himself through inner monologue in chapter seven. As he alone is capable of seeing himself from a multiple perspective, he is the most cognizant of his genius and of its relationship to the Werther experience.

Since the Werther experience is greater than the person of Goethe, the significance of chapters eight and nine can be overlooked if too much emphasis is placed on chapter seven as a climax of the novel.[106] In the first seven chapters, Goethe, the Goethe myth, and a wealth of variations in the Werther experience are presented from various perspectives. In the last two chapters, however, the reader himself provides the perspective on the basis of what has been presented in the first seven. Thus, the focal point of the Werther experience does not coincide with the focal point of Goethe, for the line of interest passes through chapter seven, diffuses in chapter eight, and refocuses at the end of chapter nine.[107] Since dynamic process rather than static achievement characterizes the Werther experience, chapter seven is an illusory climax, made ironic by entitling it—in the German edition—"The Seventh Chapter" rather than "Chapter Seven" in line with the other chapters.[108]

The basic element of the Werther experience, the common denominator of all the variations that occur in the novel, is the overcoming and synthesis of the given reality of the past and present in the present in order to move into the future with greater insight. The first seven chapters are basically about the past: the reader is informed about Goethe and the historical events of his age, from his childhood to his present. The eighth chapter represents a confrontation in the present, but it is a superficial one between the myth of Goethe's greatness and the Lotte myth. The perspective from this confrontation, however, leads to chapter nine, in which the process of synthesis in the present occurs by stripping the myth from the person, overcoming the myth, and establishing identity. The structure of the novel, therefore, represents the basic Werther experience: synthesizing all that is and has been, in synthesizing it overcoming it, and moving on to a higher level of insight. In the Kestner-Charlotte-Goethe triangle behind the original Werther experience, Goethe overcomes himself in creating and sacrificing Werther, whereby he experiences a spiritual rebirth and continues to develop on a higher plane of insight. With Goethe, this is a continual process wherein lies his greatness, his ability to synthesize all the positive and negative aspects: the powers of chaos and the powers of order within his person; the complexities, polarities, and contradictions in his character.

The Willemer-Marianne-Goethe triangle is another example of the Werther experience, but represents Goethe's later development, the outgrowth of which is *West-Eastern Divan* (1814–19). The novel thus spans from the original Werther experience to the mature Goethe at the end of the novel, a line of development which traces the dynamic process of continual spiritual rebirth. This span is reflected in the German title of the novel: *Lotte in Weimar*. The word "Lotte" is immediately associated with *The Sorrows of Young Werther* (1774) and Goethe's Storm and Stress period, and the word "Weimar" is associated with *Divan* and the mature Goethe.[109] The span is also emphasized by the quote from *Divan* with which Mann prefaces the novel and by Goethe's characterization of *Divan* and *Werther* as being "the same thing on different levels" (319).

The August-Ottilie-Ferdinand triangle represents a contrastive Werther experience, for August and Ottilie, due to the tyranny they feel in the shadow of Goethe's genius, are not acting through their own self-identities. August is but an extension of Goethe, and Ottilie is really attracted to the genius of Goethe through August. Aside from this, Ferdinand is not a Goethe-Werther equivalent, for Ottilie's renunciation of Ferdinand is without substance since he has no real interest in Ottilie. This triangle, however, serves to underscore Charlotte's inner conflict, for she fears that her own renunciation of Goethe for Kestner was equally without substance, that Goethe had merely used her for literary purposes. This fear is further underscored by August's presentation of the Willemer-Marianne-Goethe triangle, in which he portrays Goethe's relief at being out of the triangle situation. In still another variation, Goethe's presentation of the Italian singer also emphasizes Charlotte's inner conflict, for she sees parallels in this episode to her own fate as well as an admission through association by Goethe that she indeed had been the means to a literary end.

All of these variations point to Charlotte's own Werther experience. Although Goethe is the focal point of the first seven chapters, Charlotte is the only character—aside from Mager—who appears in each of the first six. It is her inner conflict of self-identity, the confusion of Charlotte and the Lotte myth which stems from the Goethe-Werther experience, that pervades these six chapters. The events of the first five chapters and the seventh occur simultaneously. They are, in effect, the crystallization points of the sphere of Goethe and the myth surrounding him and the sphere of Charlotte and the Lotte myth. Chapter six, the August chapter, picks up the ends of chapters five and seven and focuses Charlotte's Werther experience into chapter eight, the first confrontation between the two spheres. This confrontation, however, is between the Lotte myth and the Goethe myth and does nothing to solve the conflict of Charlotte's identity. It is the decisive confrontation in chapter nine between Charlotte and the Lotte myth that resolves the conflict, for here Charlotte realizes the nature of Goethe's genius, her role in the original Werther experience, and the literary expression of the experience. In a sense, Charlotte duplicates what Goethe had done by recreating Charlotte Kestner as Lotte in *Werther*. On her return from the theater in Goethe's coach, she remains for a time in the realm of art—the realm in which the finite and infinite, the potential and the real can be reconciled[110]—and recreates Goethe as a coach companion. This establishes lines of comparison between the elements which characterize Goethe's inner monologue in chapter seven and the elements of the dialogue which ensues here. Although she experiences rather than records this "literary" creation, by recreating Goethe and sacrificing the Lotte myth, she experiences a variation of the spiritual rebirth inherent in Goethe's re-creation of Charlotte and sacrificing of Werther. The title of the novel thus reflects the Werther experience of Charlotte as much as the span of development in the continual Werther experience of Goethe (different as these experiences may be) for between the Charlotte of the original Werther experience and the Charlotte in Weimar, a synthesis has occurred which offers insight on a higher level into her life and the myth which surrounds it.[111]

These variations, all more or less presented directly, point indirectly to a Werther experience of a larger context which relates the novel to Mann and his assessment of Goethe— arrived at through his study of Goethe against the influences of Schopenhauer, Nietzsche, and Wagner[112]—and to his contemporary world. Mann inextricably associates the genius of Goethe with the greatness of the German historical-cultural tradition. It is for this reason that he consciously portrays

Goethe as a personality of contradictions and polarities, a personality which embodies the powers of chaos and order, the abyss and Olympian height, whose greatness lies in the ability to synthesize these elements into a totality, for this is how he views the German historical-cultural tradition.[113]

Mann's choice of Goethe as the historical material for such a literary expression of Germany's cultural tradition signifies his own belief in and adherence to a better, truer Germany than the world was witnessing in his age.[114] His view of the German is expressed by Goethe who finds it "wretched that they abandon themselves credulously to every fanatic scoundrel who speaks to their baser qualities, confirms them in their vices, teaches them nationality means barbarism and isolation. . . . They think they are Germany—but I am. Let the rest perish root and branch, it will survive in me. Do your best to fend me off, still I stand for you" (330–31). But Mann does not wish to see the phenomenon of Germany and Germany's cultural tradition split into two Germanys, one good and one bad.[115] Instead, he wishes to present and preserve the totality and greatness of this tradition, "for that sort of Germany is freedom, is culture, universality, love" (331) and to prevent its destruction by the horrors of Nazism, which in Mann's view represents a catastrophic magnification of only certain negative elements within this totality.[116]

Mann presents a wealth of indirect references to his contemporary world that emphasize the association he draws between Goethe and contemporary Germany.[117] These references occur mainly through the utterances of characters that display the artistic genius of Mann, for the vast majority of them are taken from historically documented sources and then transformed by Mann to meet his literary needs.[118] In this transformation, they occasionally lose their validity within their historical context, but never within the fictional presentation or as the medium for Mann to express his own observations on his contemporary world. This procedure of transforming utterances from outside sources into a new context receives literary expression in the novel itself: Charlotte takes Riemer's concept of "elemental" and uses it in her own context (86–87, 272). She repeats, as if it were her own observation, Adele's comment on new writers not being able to attain the achievement of Goethe but, in a way, to surpass it (97, 264).[119]

On the most basic level of reference, one can observe that Goethe witnessed in his age political and social upheaval not dissimilar to that which Mann witnesses in his own age. Mann, however, draws sharper points of reference in a variety of forms, so that even Goethe's comment on the weather—"A changeable, contrary-minded day" (301)—becomes an indirect reference by Mann to his own world, especially if one bears in mind that *The Beloved Returns* was completed on the eve of Hitler's invasion of Poland.

In speaking of Ottilie and her ideal of the Prussian officer, Adele alludes to the masses of Nazi Germany and their relationship to the past: "Needless to say, this cult-image bore more or less clearly the traits glorified by the memory of her lost father" (147). Prussian militarism and the loss in the First World War are, in a sense, the "fallen father of Nazi Germany" and form the base of the cult of Nazism and Hitler. In commenting on the Romantics, she also points out the danger of nationalistic fervor, referring to Mann's age and the Nazis: "Enthusiasm is beautiful. But not without enlightenment. When hysterical citizens revel metaphorically in the shedding of blood, because the historic hour has given the rein to their evil passions, the sight is painful to behold" (187–88).

The inherent need in man to idolize and worship a godhead is reflected in Riemer's comment: "Obviously man cannot get on without mysteries. If he has lost his taste for the Christian ones he uplifts himself with the pagan, or the nature-mystery of personality" (69). In Mann's age, this alludes to the Nietzschean cult of the great individual through the figure of Goethe, and to the distorted form this cult assumes in regard to Hitler. The relationship between the godhead tyrant and the tyrannized becomes clearer through Adele, who maintains that Goethe dominated her salon and tyrannized society "not so much because he was a tyrant as because the others submitted to him and positively forced him into the rôle" (132). Bearing the immense qualitative differences in mind, this negatively reflects the attitude of the suppliants towards Goethe no less than the attitude of the masses towards Hitler. The theme of the godhead tyrant is connected to the crisis inherent in the sacrifice of self-identity to the godhead. Riemer can sacrifice his own identity so completely at times that the letters he writes for Goethe sound more like Goethe than Goethe himself. August is so overwhelmed by the aura of the godhead that he has no real identity of his own. Ottilie sacrifices a portion of her self to the Goethe phenomenon as well.

There are innumerable references to Goethe as a godhead who demands sacrifice.[120] Riemer compares Goethe to Proteus and speaks of the "divine ozone" which emanates from him (89). Goethe is the only one whom Adele addresses formally rather than with "uncle" or "aunt" (129–30). She also explains the necessity of keeping her salon's interest in other writers a secret from Goethe because of the First Commandment (137). Meyer prepares Goethe's guests as if they were in a temple and being readied to approach divinity (384–86). Mann's portrayal of Goethe's handling of bread and wine has obvious religious implications (401–3). As already pointed out, however, the inherent need in man to be tyrannized by a godhead is what creates the actual tyranny of the godhead. Goethe has been elevated in an aura of divinity by those around him. Those connected to Goethe have been elevated, to a certain extent, with him, but, since this elevation does not emanate from their own identities, a crisis of identity takes place, and they sacrifice at least a portion of their own identity to the myth they create. It should not be overlooked that the same phenomenon, in reduced form, characterizes Charlotte, who—as a species of visiting royalty—grants audiences to those who desire to partake in the aura of the Lotte myth.

In the case of Goethe, however, the godhead brings the greatest sacrifice. In the image of the burning candle and the moth, it is the light from the candle which attracts the moth and sacrifices it, but the candle must sacrifice itself to produce the light (451). Thus, the type of greatness and divinity associated with Goethe as well as the sacrifices made by him and those connected to him are involved in the process of the Werther experience, a process, for those who understand it, of giving and taking, of spiritual and intellectual enrichment.[121]

In regard to Nazi Germany and Hitler, the basic elements of this crisis of identity and the sacrifice of the self are manifest in a perverted form. Under Nazism, the Germans sacrificed their self-identity to the godhead they created, believing or sensing that in so doing they elevated themselves and participated in the greatness they had projected into their godhead. The very fact that one refers to the "masses" of Nazi Germany rather than to the majority of Germans under Nazism indicates this loss of self-identity, the total sacrifice of individuality to the godhead tyrant, Hitler. Hitler, however, does not bring the greatest sacrifice of all, nor are he and the masses of Nazi Germany involved in a Werther process comparable to that portrayed through Mann's Goethe.

The figure of Goethe, therefore, offers simultaneously a comparison and a contrast to Hitler. The inherent need in man to be tyrannized is fulfilled in Hitler as well as in Goethe, but since Hitler magnifies certain negative elements of the totality that Goethe represents, the aspects of tyranny and sacrifice take on an entirely different meaning.

The figure of Napoleon is also connected to the theme of tyranny but he plays a double role in the novel. On the one hand, Goethe's naïve admiration for a dictator intent on European domination obviously refers to the admiration and idolization of Hitler by the Germans. On the other hand, in Mann's presentation of Goethe's appraisal of Napoleon, he becomes for the historical-cultural tradition of France what Goethe becomes for the historical-cultural tradition of Germany. Goethe saw himself not so much in nationalistic terms but as a representative of a supranational culture,[122] and it is for the sake of culture *per se* that Mann wishes to preserve the totality of Germany's cultural tradition rather than for any nationalistic goal.[123]

In regard to France, the special relationship between the cultural lives of France and Germany need hardly be recalled. In this light the relationship between Goethe and Napoleon in the novel must be seen, and Goethe's appraisal and admiration of Napoleon understood (162). In the last analysis and perhaps somewhat ironically, the element of naïveté prevails in the case of Goethe as well as in the case of Mann, for Napoleon did not actually represent what Goethe supposed, nor did Mann's idea of a supranationalistic post-war Europe materialize.[124]

Other references to Mann's contemporary world include

Adele's characterization of Monsieur Denon, Napoleon's In-
spector General of the Imperial Museums, as "art-advisor in the
appropriation of works of art in the conquered countries" (159),
alluding to the plunder of Europe's art treasures by the Nazis;
and August's account of Voss's attack on patriot pietists and
neo-Catholics, "whose glorification of the past was nothing but
spiteful defamation of the present" (271), which reflects the
Nazi falsification and glorification of Germany's history.

Through Goethe's tale of persecution of the Jews, his praise
for the great contribution of the Jews to the culture of the world,
and his comparison between the Jews and the Germans
(410–17), Mann makes reference to the situation of the Jews in
his own age and points out the irrationality and the cruel irony
behind such persecution. Mann's own concern and fears for the
Germans as well as for the Jews in what could result from the
contemporary catastrophe in Germany are expressed when he
has Goethe admit "that sometimes he was conscious of a fear
that almost took away his breath lest one day the concentrated
world hatred against that other salt of the earth, the German
stock, would be released in a historic uprising of which that
mediaeval night of butchery was but a rehearsal in miniature"
(417). This prophetic fear was only half realized, for an anti-
German sentiment did prevail throughout and long after the
war, but was not expressed in the form of the persecution that
the Jews in Goethe's tale or in twentieth-century Germany
suffered.

Equally broad references are made to exile and the artist in
exile. The most obvious reference is Goethe's traveling to Töp-
litz in Bohemia to escape the theater of war while Napoleon's
troops were being driven back (126–27). More pointed references are made through Goethe's inner monologue and his
thoughts on the Germans, thoughts through which Mann
speaks for his own age: "Fate will smite them, for betraying
themselves and not wanting to be what in fact they are. She will
scatter them over the earth like the Jews, and justly. For their
best always lived in exile among them; and in exile only, in
dispersion, will they develop all the good there is in them for
healing of the nations, and become the salt of the earth . . ."
(339). In this one utterance, Mann alludes not only to exile, to
the generalized cause which necessitates exile, to a parallel

between the traditional fate of the Jews and the fate of his own contemporaries forced into exile, but also to the positive effects he hopes will result from exile in preserving the totality of the German cultural tradition for the world.

Two more references deserve mention, because they reflect on Mann's writing of the novel itself. The first—presented through August's comments on art and politics (267)—alludes to Mann's change in political stance as an artist, brought about by the rise of Nazism and the phenomenon of exile. Although an artist is never really disassociated from political events, since they form an integral part of the reality from which an artist creates, he is rarely actively engaged in them. The historical events of Mann's age were of such import, however, that they demanded from Mann a change from this relatively apolitical stance to one in which the political events could not be divorced from his literary work. Granting this, the second reference reveals that Mann is too great an artist to allow the mere expression of timely historical events to overwhelm the timeless qualities of a work of art. With a great deal of irony he comments on himself and his novel when he has Goethe reflect on *Werther*: "Blood goes to my head when I think of all the young popinjay dragged in, in his frenzied search for motivation: social rebellion, offended bourgeois pride—why did you have to bring that in, young simpleton, a bit of political tinder that takes away from the whole thing? . . . A good thing nobody paid it much heed, just swallowed it along with the other fiery excesses and felt sure it was not meant for direct effect. Silly, immature stuff, moreover subjectively fake" (320). Both Goethe and Mann were indeed spontaneously affected by these very elements; but, since they are subordinated to the totality of the novels as works of art, they in no way alter the validity of the artistic expression for posterity, contrary to any criticism which Goethe received and which Mann foresaw.[125]

To return once again to the central core of the novel, the Werther experience, and to look at it in terms of the novel as an entity, the deeper significance behind the quote from *Divan* which prefaces the novel can be seen. Goethe's Werther experience on a higher level of insight is reflected in *Divan*, and central to that work is a wealth of allusions and the treatment of serious and grave material in a light but sincere manner. This is, in effect, exactly what Mann presents in his own way in *The Beloved Returns*, "a joyousness replete with wisdom, a smiling earnestness that is all lightness in form but weighty in deep and mysterious implications.[126]

Hermann Broch
The Death of Virgil

The Death of Virgil[127] is a prime example of the extent to which Calliope can create epic art from the most meager offerings of Clio. Broch utilizes exiguous fragments of historical fact[128] surrounding the death of Virgil to question the value and viability of literature in an age of crisis. This limited theme, however, is broadened to universal dimensions, namely the cognition and resolution of the myriad contradictions of existence, in which existence becomes a totality: life and death, heaven and hell, past and future, inner and outer, finite and infinite, rational and irrational, the individual and collective humanity form a closed ring with neither beginning nor end.[129]

The plot of the novel is a mere skeleton, for Broch internalizes the content, replacing epic breadth with depth. In relating the meager plot to the central theme of the novel, however, two climaxes become apparent: the resolve to burn the *Aeneid* and the sudden decision not to. The content of the novel, therefore, is concerned with processes rather than with plot, for it is only through analyzing the processes which lead to these two climaxes that the novel can be understood. And it is exactly these processes, the process of cognition and the process of resolution, which are expressed in the totality of the novel.[130]

The process leading to the resolve to destroy the *Aeneid* begins with Virgil's arrival in Brundisium. Virgil is the greatest poet of his age and is about to finish a poetic edifice acclaimed as the counterpart to Caesar Augustus's political edifice: Imperial Rome. His nearness to death, however, sharply tunes his perception of self and his life's work. He closes his eyes to the stench and obscenities as he is borne to the imperial palace. He cannot suppress the growing intuitive feeling that he, the poet who had striven to see life as a whole, who had seen his mission as unifying in art the fragmentation of a world in crisis, had failed. Just as he closes his eyes to the reality in the streets, he senses he has filtered out part of reality in his art. He begins to see the *Aeneid* not as resolving the imperfection inherent in all things, but as the supreme symbol of that very imperfection. This sense of failure is intensified by the drunken scene Virgil witnesses from his window, a scene which ends in nihilistic cosmic laughter. To Virgil's horror, this laughter blends with other sounds to produce a harmony of beauty. This too he relates to the *Aeneid,* and again he cannot suppress the feeling that he has created a thing of beauty indifferent to good and evil, devoid of responsibility to reality, a work devoid of human love. For him, the *Aeneid* represents the greatest fraud: beauty of this nature in an age of crisis is a mortal sin, for this beauty evades human involvement, duty, and love. He is then plunged into a visionary state in which a voice from within commands him to repudiate his past entirely, a command embodied in the words "Burn the *Aeneid!*" (178), which marks the end of the process leading to the first climax.

The process leading to the second climax, the decision not to burn the *Aeneid,* is revealed first in a vision of Virgil's subconscious and then in the reality of the encounter between Virgil and Augustus. Virgil awakes after the imperative to burn the *Aeneid,* conscious of a supreme sacrifice. But the destruction of the *Aeneid* is not the supreme sacrifice demanded to heal the world's ills. Therefore, his resolve to sacrifice it is not translated immediately into action. Instead, Virgil again enters the realm of vision where the ethical imperative of love is revealed to him: love as the instrument for making the world whole again, love as embodied in the bringer of salvation, love expressed in a pure sacrifice to re-establish the covenant between man and the divine. Virgil, then, witnesses the first intuition of salvation to come, but he is neither the herald nor the bringer of this salvation. He awakens to the imperative, "Open your eyes to Love!" (221).

What transpired on the subconscious level of vision now transpires on the conscious level of inner reality in the encounter with Augustus, an encounter between infinite and finite reality. Augustus defines reality in terms of the State, Virgil in terms of the Kingdom to Come; Augustus sees piety as subservience to the State, Virgil as cognition in love which transcends death; Augustus speaks and acts in terms of finite totalitarianism, Virgil in terms of the ultimate reality of total cognition. Unable to comprehend Virgil, Augustus bursts into a rage, which marks the climax of the second process, for it causes Virgil to recognize for the first time a fellow human being rather than the embodiment of the finite State, and Virgil is moved by compassionate love in human fellowship. In the single moment of sensing this love, the finite and the infinite worlds are united. Having opened his eyes to love, Virgil is stripped of all selfishness. He is therefore free to act selflessly: He gives the *Aeneid* to Augustus and requests the right to free his slaves.

Virgil, in vision and in reality, has gained insight into the world to come, the transition from the pagan to the Christian Age. Just as he is granted the first intuition of future salvation, he is granted in death the first intuition of the spiritual rebirth this salvation signifies.[131] This spiritual rebirth is reflected in part four of the novel, in the process of cosmic creation in reverse, the reunion with the godhead in primeval darkness, and in the re-enactment of creation. That which was at the beginning, namely the Word, is that which stands at the end of the novel, "Speech," symbolic expression of the inexpressible.

This resolution of past, present, and future, of life and death, is the basic concept in the structure of the novel: "One thought, one moment, one sentence."[132] To achieve this totality, Broch employs lyrical language and musical form as the only means capable of such an expression, for the inexpressible cannot occur through the rational content of words, but only through the irrational tension between words, word phrases, sentence structures, and the flow within and through each other.[133] This totality of expression is clearly visible in the most superficial aspects of the language Broch employs, especially in the verbal constructions which combine infinitive, present participle, and past participle forms of a single verb, thus transcending all temporality.[134]

The physical structure of the novel is also an expression of totality in the process of cognition and resolution. The four parts ("Water—The Arrival," "Fire—The Descent," "Earth—The Expectation," and "Air—The Homecoming") define the order, direction, and space within which cognition and resolution take place and correspond to the cognitive processes of Virgil.[135] Water and earth, arrival and expectation, represent a horizontal line which relates to the interassociations of sleep, love, and death and which correspond to Virgil's phases of conscious reality. Fire and air, descent and homecoming, represent a vertical line which relates to the cognitive range of man from beast to god, from the Dionysian to the Apollonian, and corresponds to Virgil's phases of subconscious reality. The self of man is the axis where both lines intersect, making possible an infinite range of cognition. In the realm of conscious reality, the self may share equally in the range of the vertical line, or it may devolute or evolute along the cognitive range of the vertical.

What is expressed in the novel, then, is the expansion of the self, in the example of Virgil, in all directions along both the vertical and the horizontal lines. The four parts of the novel are literally movements in this expansion, stages or variations in the levels of cognition, which culminate in the last part, in the last word, "Speech," as the ultimate word-symbol for expressing the simultaneity and totality of existence. Therefore, the novel is symphonic in structure:[136] the four parts of the novel constituting four movements of a verbal symphony, each movement a variation of the central theme of cognition, the totality of which is resolved in the final chord, in a single moment of total cognition of ultimate reality.

The relationship that exists between the novel and Broch's contemporary world is expressed in the first instance in a limited identification between Broch and Virgil.[137] Through his brief but intensely experienced imprisonment by the Gestapo in 1938, Broch is confronted with the very real possibility of his own death and begins to see his previous Virgil material in light of his own life and age: "It was no longer the death of Virgil, it became the imagining of my own dying."[138] Therefore, when Broch uses the word "poet" in connection with the novel, he refers specifically to himself and generally to the writer of his age, expressed in the figure of Virgil, "for although it is presented in the third person, it is an inner monologue of the poet. It is therefore, above all else, a coming to terms with his own life, with the moral correctness or incorrectness of this life, with the justification and non-justification of the poetic endeavors to which his life was dedicated."[139]

This identification is also present in the theme of exile, which is inextricably connected to the figure of Virgil, who, having lost the family estate in Mantua in the Perusinic War, went to Athens. In addition, Broch prefaces his novel with quotes from the *Aeneid* and from Dante's *Divine Comedy*, drawing attention to the fact that Dante, too, was an exile. Perhaps of even greater importance is the fact that Virgil's hero Aeneas is an exile, fleeing from the burning Troy in search of a new homeland.[140]

A more significant relationship between the novel and Broch's contemporary world lies in the material itself. At the heart of the Virgil material is the legend of Virgil's resolve to burn the *Aeneid*. Broch recognized "that a spirit such as Virgil's was not driven to such despair for trivial reasons, but that the entire historical and metaphysical substance of the epoch was implicated."[141] It is the recognition of an existential crisis in man and the failure to resolve that crisis in the *Aeneid* that encourage Broch's Virgil to destroy his work. At the center of this crisis is the loss of human fellowship in a community of man. He has become an isolated unit of a mass civilization and is left exposed to the threatening forces of existence. In such a state, man willingly accepts, indeed demands, subjugation to a higher authority. Caesar Augustus recognizes this in the "gigantic masses without judgment," who "follow anyone who is clever enough to wrap himself in the glittering and seductive mantle of freedom," but "they know it for a sham freedom whereby they are turned into a frightened, veering, leaderless herd" (365). Augustus sees Imperial Rome as fulfilling a necessary existential function by providing a structure which defines the limits of existence and offers a type of security. This, however, represents a finite solution to an infinite crisis. The existential crisis of man is thus embodied in the totalitarianism of Imperial Rome; the elevation of the finite State to the infinite; the elevation of the mortal, Augustus, to a godhead; the subjugation of the masses to this godhead. Revealing the historical and metaphysical content of this existential crisis in Virgil's age is the medium by which Broch reveals the historical and metaphysical content of the existential crisis of his own age. This crisis made concrete in Imperial Rome has its counterpart in the totalitarian regimes of Broch's age, the most destructive of which are Fascism and Communism. As symbolized by Augustus and the masses in the novel, the mass insanity in such modern totalitarian regimes is a reflection of the heightened need in man to seek existential security by subjugating himself to a higher authority.

The manifestation of mass insanity and the evil it embodies in the immediate oppression of Nazism is clearly portrayed in the novel, especially in the arrival of Caesar Augustus in Brundisium, "which the brooding mass-beast had awaited to release its howl of joy, and now it broke loose, without pause, without end, victorious, violent, unbridled, fear-inspiring, magnificent, fawning, the mass worshipping itself in the person of the One" (22). This clearly alludes to the insanity of the German masses in regard to their god-head, Hitler. It is this mass insanity and Broch's own imprisonment that revealed to him the potential for evil embodied in man collectively. He recognizes "the people's profound capacity for evil in all its ramifications, their possibilities for human degradation in becoming a mob, and their reversion therewith to the anti-human" (23).

Broch, however, is not merely dealing with the immediate manifestations of the catastrophe of his age, namely Hitler and Nazism. Instead, he penetrates to the causes behind these manifestations, to the roots of modern man's existential crisis, for which Nazism is but a symptomatic expression. This underlying cause is "the hollowing out of existence" (23) which transforms man into a member of a "mob, in which, lacking a common perception, none loves the other, none helps the other, none comprehends the other, none trusts the other" (133). This describes the loss of a meaningful existential core in modern man. To fill this void, man seeks a higher authority by mythologizing the powers which determine his existence. In the case of modern man, this no longer involves mythologizing the powers of nature, but rather the powers of reason as embodied in science and technology, the authority from which man expects to dispel the insecurities of his existence.[142]

Broch comes to the conclusion that it is Marxism today, just as it was the idea behind Imperial Rome in Virgil's age, that sees itself filling the void in this existential crisis, and that Fascism is but a mere imitation, in nationalistic form, of Marxism.[143] Here, as there, these forms of totalitarianism represent attempts to make the finite infinite, to elevate the fascist or communist State to the ultimate determinant of existence, to which man the mass bows in subjugation.

Against this totalitarianism, Broch issues an ethical call to resist all tendencies to enslave man, the ultimate expression of which he sees in the Nazi concentration camps: "Man is stripped of the last vestiges of individuality; instead of a name he receives a number and is to perceive of himself only as a number. He has become a corpse before he has died, and whether he starves or freezes, whether he succumbs to untreated wounds and infirmities or is executed, he experiences his suffering as and like an animal, without farewell, for he possesses nothing more of the world. Even the magic of being completely at mercy, the magic of contrition is extinguished; what was once a man has become sub-animal, scarcely even vegetable, a numerical corpse, rubbish which still moans.[144]

In the novel, the ethical call to resistance is translated into the ethical act of Virgil freeing his slaves. This act embodies the call to spiritual rebirth as exemplified in Virgil's first intuitive glimpse of the Kingdom to Come and in the retro-enactment and re-enactment of Genesis. It is a call to the single earthly duty of man, "the duty of helpfulness, the duty of awakening; there was no other duty, and even man's duty toward divinity and the god's duty toward humanity consisted of nothing other than helpfulness" (132). It is a call to love, to re-establish a genuine fellowship of man.

The task of the artist is to contribute to this awakening to reality through his artistic medium. Virgil sees this as his failing when he cries out in a moment of self-knowledge that he "had not so much described as tried to glorify" (22) in his *Aeneid*, and this forms the question which Broch poses concerning the value and viability of literature in an age of crisis. What is revealed by Broch through Virgil is "that the duty of all art lay . . . in the self-perceived finding and proclaiming of truth, the duty which has been laid on the artist, so that the soul, realizing the great equilibrium between the ego and the universe, might recover herself in the universe" (139). *The*

Death of Virgil, then, provides an answer to the challenge of Broch's age by countering the tendency towards totalitarianism with an all-encompassing view of reality.[145] He counters the reduction of the infinite to the finite with the revelation of the infinite in the finite. Just as Virgil stands at the threshold of the Christian age, preceded by an age of disintegration of human values, Broch sees modern man again at the threshold of a new age, preceded by the greatest disintegration of human values, embodied in the horrors of Nazism.

3

Conclusion

On the basis of the individual studies in this cross section of historical novels, certain conclusions can be drawn concerning the genre as a whole as it relates to the exiled authors and the age in which they lived. First of all, one should recognize that all of the novels are indeed historical novels, a fact which may require some rethinking on the part of literary scholars. Literary critics and readers in general are not justified in dictating to a literary artist how he may or may not use historical material for a literary work of art; such material is the creative medium of the artist. In regard to literature as an art form, therefore, the only legitimate criterion for defining a historical novel in the context of twentieth-century German exile is the utilization of history as source material.[1]

The cross section of historical novels treated here reveals the wide range possible in such use. The order in which the novels were discussed reflects a progression from relative objectivity to relative subjectivity in the treatment of the material. The wealth of historically documented facts in Cordan's material contrasts sharply with the scarcity of the same in Broch's. This represents a contrast of materials and the author's use of them, however, rather than any substantive contrast in terms of artistic expression. This is underscored by the fact that the next two works at either end of the spectrum, Frank's *Cervantes* and

Thomas Mann's *The Beloved Returns*, reveal to a certain extent exactly the opposite in regard to historical documentation. Since artistic expression presupposes subjectivity on the part of the artist, objectivity and subjectivity are entirely relative in regard to historical accuracy.[2] In regard to literature as a creative art form, moreover, the question of objectivity is completely irrelevant.

Without exception, all of the novels bear reference to the contemporary world of the authors. Indeed, it seems curious to suppose that they could do otherwise. Significant art always has been and presumably always will be the most sublime perception of the artist's world, and any writer who views himself as a literary artist and his work as literary art cannot but deal with his contemporary world. This does not imply that all historical novels written in exile are works of art—far from it—but it is inconceivable that a historical novel could succeed as a literary work of art and not be concerned with the contemporary world in some significant manner.

The individual studies indicate that there is a direct relationship between the historical material used and the references made to the contemporary world. The progression from relative objectivity to relative subjectivity describes a trend rather than an absolute demarcation, for there are direct as well as indirect references to the contemporary world in all of the novels. The tendency clearly indicates, however, that the two ends of the objective-subjective spectrum lend themselves best to indirect reference, whereas the center of the spectrum lends itself to direct reference. The example of Feuchtwanger, however, reveals the inherent danger in making references which are too direct, for the literary quality of such a work clearly suffers. This is demonstrated in a comparison of Feuchtwanger's novel with the two adjacent novels, those of Maass and Heinrich Mann. Both approach the directness of Feuchtwanger's novel but from opposite ends of the objective-subjective spectrum; the direct references do not overwhelm the novel itself as a work of art.

Previous studies on the German historical novel in exile have made literary value judgments on the basis of the directness or indirectness of reference to the author's contemporary world.[3] This type of value judgment is invalid in literary terms, for it is not literary at all, but political or ideological. This approach, however, has been applied far too broadly in viewing and evaluating the historical novels of the German exiles, both during the period of exile and today. This lies at the root of the controversy at the beginning of the exile period and is responsible for the plethora of non-literary evaluations—of individual works and authors or of the genre as a whole—that have thus far been produced.

This non-literary tendency is clearly evident in the misinterpretations, one-sided approaches, and omissions in previous studies of the genre. With the exception of studies of Heinrich Mann, Thomas Mann, and Broch, few attempts have been made to approach the novels included in this study as literature. The results have been curious. Feuchtwanger's The Pretender was until recently acclaimed as a significant historical novel, whereas in fact it is one of the weakest. Cordan, Frank, and Maass have been virtually ignored. Neumann and Roth have been charged with avoiding the real concerns of their age, a charge which this study refutes entirely. The historical novels of Heinrich Mann, Döblin, Thomas Mann, and Broch, established names in twentieth-century German literature, have usually been treated with deference, but, as this study shows, often for the wrong reasons in regard to particular works.

The task of the literary critic is to fashion critical tools for dealing with a particular period of literary history or development, to create some type of order in a mass of material, and to define basic characteristics or tendencies. These tasks have not been carried out in the critical treatment of the German historical novel in exile. The phenomenal number of historical novels written in exile and the predominantly non-literary approaches taken thus far in evaluations of the genre warrant such an attempt at ordering and defining this mass of material. Such classifications, definitions, and typologies, however, are critical crutches at best: the lines of demarcation are fluid and not absolute.

In a review of the cross section of historical novels analyzed in this study, certain characteristics and tendencies do become clear which can aid the literary critic in discussing and evaluating the historical novel in exile. Since the authors writing in exile were influenced in their literary production by the diverse movements in which they had participated and experienced in Germany—ranging from the later stages of Naturalism and Impressionism, through Neo-Romanticism and Neo-Classicism, to Expressionism and the New Objectivity—there are characteristics which the authors have in common as well as stylistic differences which separate them.

An indebtedness to Neo-Romanticism and a basic humanist attitude are common to all of the authors. The degree of indebtedness and the nature of the attitude, however, are as varied as the authors themselves. The Neo-Romantics' use of history to present universal human values, to offer heroic models for contemporary man, and to reflect the problems of the modern world is paralleled in the historical novel in exile.[4] This particular utilization of history in the exile period, however, does not represent a conscious attempt to resurrect Neo-Romanticism. Instead, the significance of the historical novel for the exile period, and for the twentieth century in general, is an inevitable outcome of the historical events of the day and the phenomenon of exile. The fates of the exiled writers and the historical events of their age were initially experienced on an immediate, personal level. Totalitarianism, mass insanity, persecution, imprisonment, execution, exile: these are the elements of the very personal existential crisis of each writer.[5] They were unwilling to view their own fate and experience as unique in the history of mankind, hence the phenomenal rise in popularity of the historical novel precisely in this period of history. The writers seek parallels to their own situations, historical examples of similar ages and fates, in order to come to terms with the crisis in their own existence. Broch's experience is representative for the exile in general: it was his own imprisonment and nearness to death that caused him to view historical material in light of his immediate situation.[6]

In doing so these writers recognized that their situation and fates were indeed not unique, that history shows many eras which exhibited similar phenomena. While these writers undoubtedly took personal comfort in this awareness, they also viewed their own fates and their age in a larger historical context. Through the examples and parallels discovered in history, the contemporary expressions of totalitarianism, mass

insanity, persecution, and exile come to be viewed as symptomatic magnifications of an existential crisis of modern man
in general. The exile writers found that the historical examples
invariably occurred at turning points in history, in ages of
transitions. It is not surprising, therefore, that the majority of
historical novels written in exile, and all of those treated in this
study, utilize historical figures and material drawn from such
ages: Julian, Cervantes, Struensee, Don Pedro, Varro, Henri
Quatre, Cuzumarra, Las Casas, and Klinkert, Napoleon and
Angelina, Goethe and Lotte, Virgil and Augustus.

The exiles recognized that such an age of transition witnesses
a clash between an established order of existence and a newly
emerging order. In the historical examples, these orders were
religious, social, and/or political, and represented the existential authority from which man derived the meaning and security for his existence. In such a confrontation, the authority
of the established order is placed in question; existential security and the meaning of life are threatened. This is expressed
in the clashes between Constantius and Julian, indirectly between Cervantes and Philip II, between Struensee and the
Danish Court, between sixteenth-century Spain and the Age of
Humanism in Maass, between Augustus and Virgil, and among
the multiple examples in Döblin. In the twentieth century it is
the clash between the authority of orthodox religious structures—which, as presented by Döblin, have lost their
viability—and the authority of science and technology—which
have failed to provide a viable substitute. This confrontation of
orders produces an existential crisis in man, for there is no
longer an unquestioned authority through which man can define his existence, find security, or give meaning to life. This
condition results in the emergence of the Messianic Idea, an
attempt to find a new authority.

This Messianic Idea is the major element that the writers
recognize in the historical events of their own age. The rise of
totalitarian dictatorships and the evil embodied in them are
basically an expression of man's Messianic expectation. But the
Messiah figures and the orders established by these figures are
clearly opposed to humanity. Through historical examples, the
exiled writers show how modern man's existential crisis comes
to be embodied in such anti-humanistic Messiah figures and

such negative and evil Messianic social structures. Their novels reveal the root cause for this development to be the inability of man to recognize the nature of his existential crisis, to recognize that it basically belongs in the realm of the infinite. As a result, man tends to seek a solution in the realm of the finite and to accord it the aspects of the infinite, turning the mundane into an absolute, turning human leaders into gods, creating myths to imbue the finite order with the aura of the divine.

All of the novels reveal these tendencies. In Cordan, the masses are liberated from the tyranny of Constantius but are eager to worship Julian as the Messiah, a role he rejects. In Frank, the masses are incapable of recognizing their condition, just as Catalina finds her sole reality in the super-heros of the *Amadis* fantasies. In Neumann and Heinrich Mann, the masses follow whoever holds the reins of power. In Maass, the masses mistake gold for God. In Feuchtwanger, the masses blindly follow the puppet, Nero. In Döblin, the search for the Land Without Death remains in the realm of the finite for the masses. In Roth and Thomas Mann, man cannot distinguish between myth and reality. In Broch, the masses worship Augustus who himself sees finite Imperial Rome as infinite.

In all of these cases, making the finite infinite leads to evil and destruction. The reason for this inheres in the particular manner in which the masses unconsciously conceptualize the Messianic Idea. It is the expectation that a Messiah figure appears and brings salvation to man, the basic concept in the Judeo-Christian tradition. Although the exile writers embrace the Messianic Idea, they reject the idea of a Messianic figure, for they basically agree that salvation for modern man—as far as that word is even applicable—can only come from within. This is the basis for the exiles' humanist attitude and the message they offer to twentieth-century man. This message is essentially a call for a spiritual rebirth of man, based on ethical, humanist precepts, as evoked through the models from the past in their historical novels.

The horrors of German Fascism, then, are viewed as the result of modern man's misdirected attempts to resolve his existential crisis. Ironically, Hitler was indeed the embodiment of the *Zeitgeist*, for the existential crisis of modern man produced the acute desire for authoritative leadership, any leadership, to give order, any order, to man's existence. The thematic emphasis on slavery, persecution, banishment, and exile, however, reveals the actual as well as the symbolic fate of modern man in this crisis which reduced man to man as mass, a number, a commodity.

Although the conclusions drawn thus far cannot be applied directly to every historical novel written in exile, these tendencies are nevertheless characteristic. This is true even of those historical novels of lesser literary quality and of those whose primary purpose is to further a particular political or ideological cause. In the latter case, a curious variation must be noted, however, in regard to the Messianic Idea. Those authors writing from a Marxist perspective would concur with the discussion above, including the rejection of a Messianic figure. In its place, however, appears the State as the embodiment of the Messianic Idea. These writers overlook the fact that the nature of totalitarian states per se, and not a particular one, perpetuates the existential crisis of modern man.

Although the basic attitude of these exiled writers is humanist, it is a type of humanism conditioned by the phenomenon of exile, especially in regard to the humanist concept of man's freedom to act, freedom to choose and exercise free will. Cast out of their natural sphere of influence—the culture, language, and socio-political structures to which they were accustomed and which molded their lives and values—the exiles found themselves condemned to inaction. Therefore, the figures they portray in their novels are also unable to act directly in the events of history. Julian and Henri Quatre are the exceptions. Even they, however, experience enlightenment and spiritual rebirth only on a personal level and cannot transfer it to the masses they lead as long as the masses see in them a Messianic figure expected to bring salvation from without.

The other examples of enlightenment and spiritual rebirth occur in individuals who are not in a position to act directly. Cervantes' direct actions are ineffective; only through his pen is he able to act indirectly. Don Pedro attempts to act directly by dedicating his life to the Indians, but this too is ineffective. Klinkert is overwhelmed by events to such a degree that direct action is futile from the beginning. The Werther experience occurs on the personal level and has no direct influence on the course of outside events. Virgil realizes that his insight cannot affect any direct change in the views of Augustus.

Not only did the exiles recognize the impossibility of direct action, they also questioned the effectiveness of indirect action through literary attempts to enlighten. Cordan's portrayal of the limited influence of truth, Cervantes' realization that truth would only be recognized "someday," Struensee's acknowledgement that his attempts came too soon, Bruno's contention that he has called five hundred years too soon, Virgil's realization that he alone has been granted the intuitive glimpse of the Kingdom to Come and cannot apply his insight to the world of Imperial Rome: all of these examples clearly indicate that the exiles feared that their insights would not influence modern man, an attitude confirmed, for the most past, by the reading and evaluation of their works during the exile period and up to the present day. The humanist attitude of the exiles, therefore, is a Humanism of Entrenchment.

Although the elements which the authors have in common are important, the stylistic tendencies which separate them are equally important. The first of these tendencies can be characterized as Inductive Realism, a special form and continuation in exile of the New Objectivity. The term "inductive" is used to denote the fact that the basic objective-realistic approach is twice removed from the reality the authors are portraying, first through the use of historical rather than contemporary material, secondly through the historical circumstances which prevented direct contact with and a direct relationship to the realities inside Germany.

In this group are Heinrich Mann, Bruno Frank, Robert Neumann, and, to a lesser degree, Lion Feuchtwanger. In the novels of these authors, man is portrayed as a creature determined by the basic drives: love-hate, greed-generosity, compassion-cruelty. They see man shaped by suprapersonal forces, against which the individual is powerless, but which can be comprehended objectively and countered by the organized mass. Therefore, there is little concern for metaphysics. Instead, the major concern is a direct portrayal of socio-political reform for the betterment of the masses. This attempt to reform is expressed as direct political involvement in Mann and Neumann and as frustrated individual action in Frank. Henri Quatre,

Struensee, and Cervantes all attempt to reform mankind. In Feuchtwanger, the element of reform is presented only indirectly and superficially.

Especially important in Mann, Neumann, and Feuchtwanger is the belief that reason has a decisive impact on the course of events. Central to all is a belief in progress within historical processes, the belief that historical progress is inevitable. Because attempts to reform are frustrated, however, a basic mood of scepticism, disillusionment, and resignation prevails in these novels.

A major stylistic element is the impressionistic use of multiple divisions and short scenes, each of which presents a single image in a larger picture of life. In Mann and Neumann, this tendency approaches a film mosaic technique, while in Feuchtwanger it serves mainly to divide the material. Connected to this is an emphasis on description of concrete social problems. Frank and Neumann, for example, portray socio-political conditions of the masses directly.

The tendency in all the novels to analyze or dissect the prevailing situation of man is particularly apparent in the use of conversation. In Mann, this occurs mainly through directly presented dialogues or descriptions of dialogues. In Frank, Neumann, and Feuchtwanger, there is a combination of dialogues and inner monologues. Because of the dominant objective-realistic approach of these authors, the emphasis in these discussions is on the socio-psychological rather than on depth psychology.

The second major stylistic tendency which emerges in this study can be characterized as Neoteric Romanticism. This term is used to denote a basic Romantic approach in a twentieth-century context, which includes the influences of Post-Expressionism, Existentialism, and depth psychology. Included in this group are Alfred Döblin, Joseph Roth, Edgar Maass, and Wolfgang Cordan.

The picture of man as portrayed by these authors grants the determination of man's being by suprapersonal forces, but rejects the idea that man is determined solely by basic drives, that the individual is powerless. They reject the idea that these forces can be comprehended and controlled solely by objective, rational means. Instead, they emphasize the dual nature of man. Man is influenced by rational as well as irrational forces; man is an individual but also a part of a collective; man is earthly but also part of a greater existence.

In the modern world of technology and mechanization, however, man has lost the mythical-mystical relationship to existence which alone can bridge the gap between the two poles in this dual nature. This is the basis for the existential crisis portrayed by these authors and for the metaphysical emphasis of the novels as well. Man is portrayed as existentially isolated to the point of nihilism. Roth, for example, succeeds in expressing this isolation even in the structure of the novel. But out of this existential despair emerges belief born of the rediscovery of a mythical-mystical relationship to existence.

This return of metaphysics is reflected in the myths these authors create. These are myths in a modern sense and are not to be associated with the mythicization of the finite world, which the authors recognize as the root cause of modern man's existential crisis. In Döblin, it is the Amazon which forms the nucleus of the myth; in Roth, it is the subjective portrayal of Napoleon; in Maass, the rejuvenation of Parsifal; and in Cordan, Julian. Because of the metaphysical nature of these novels, the major figures are all god-seekers, but not in the same sense. The mythical-mystical emphasis common to Romantic tendencies is invariably associated with Catholicism: this is also true of some of these Neoteric Romantics. In Roth and Maass, for example, this association with Catholicism is expressed directly. Napoleon's conversion and Don Pedro's Parsifal experience are typical of god-seekers in the Christian sense. In Döblin, Klinkert's love for Maria is an indirect expression of this connection to Catholicism; thus Klinkert is a god-seeker in a Christian sense as well. In Cordan, the search is consciously diverted from the Christian godhead, and thus Julian is a god-seeker in a non-orthodox sense.

The metaphysics and mythical-mystical relationships presented in these novels are related to depth psychology in that surface reality is penetrated to reveal what lies at its base. This is expressed stylistically in myriad ways: the indirect explication of myths themselves in Döblin and Cordan; the manner in which dreams and visions are utilized in all of the novels; the

concrete portrayal of subconscious or supraconscious realities—the debate with Bruno, for example, or the initiation rites
in Cordan. The creation of myths on the one hand and the
explication, and thus destruction, of myths through depth psychology on the other do not constitute an actual contradiction,
for the modern myths created by these authors are symbolic
representations of the realities revealed by depth psychology.
As such, symbols play a dominant stylistic role in all of the
novels, so much so that the novels could also be characterized
as Neo-Symbolist in nature.

The third major stylistic tendency is a form of Modern Classicism. Included under this rubric are Thomas Mann and Hermann Broch, who, like Schiller and Goethe, approach this
classicism from opposite poles. Stylistically, Mann is clearly
connected to Inductive Realism, Broch to Neoteric Romanticism. Their classical tendency, however, is expressed in an
emphasis on form, proportion, totality, and synthesis. In both,
form and content become a totality, for the form of their novels
is the ultimate expression of the content. Broch's symphonic
structure and language are expressions of the unity and totality
of existence. The structure of Mann's *The Beloved Returns* is
itself an expression of the Werther experience. Synthesis is the
core of the Werther experience and the heart of Virgil's insight
into the totality of existence. Broch's language is a synthesis of
past, present, and future to form a unity of expression. In
addition, a synthesis of past and present is evoked through the
invisible arc which connects Goethe and Virgil to the contemporary world.

Equally classical is the awareness of the role of literature as
an art form. Both Mann and Broch reject the idea that literature
has a political function. On the other hand, they also reject the
idea that literature is an end in itself. This is expressed on two
levels. In *The Beloved Returns*, Goethe's works are expressions
of the Werther experience but not the Werther experience itself,
and in Broch's novel, the *Aeneid* is not the totality that Virgil
seeks and finally experiences. On the second level, Mann and
Broch do not see their portrayals of Goethe and Virgil as ends in
themselves, for literature as an art form is not, in itself, the
reality it reveals. This reflection of realities removed from the

immediacy of life is the role literature plays, for only then can it reveal the greater meaning and significance of existence which the stark realities of everyday life obscure.

These three categories are merely critical aids used to demonstrate dominant stylistic tendencies within the German historical novel in exile. Though relevant and useful for the purposes of this initial approach, they will certainly be modified and remodified as the historical distance from the subject increases. Only now can we begin to view the exile period from such a distance. The belief advanced by the exiled German writers in their historical novels—that modern man is enduring an age of crisis and yet is on the threshold of a new age—is still very much a part of contemporary thought.

Who rules then over the German historical novel in exile after 1933, Calliope or Clio? The answer must be Calliope, and perhaps critics should ask themselves if this has not always been true for the entire genre when viewed as a literary art form. This in no way diminishes the role that Clio has and always will play in historical fiction. As daughters of Mnemosyne, goddess of remembrance, both Calliope and Clio are concerned with establishing order and continuity in the world by documenting the past. Both wish to serve the cause in the search for truth. As common as these endeavors are, however, they approach their goals from opposite poles. Calliope strives for subjective truth, Clio for objective; however, just as Calliope makes use of Clio's province, so Clio cannot escape the influence of Calliope in interpreting historical facts. They serve, therefore, equally important complementary functions for the human psyche and the body of knowledge. The truth revealed by Clio is never complete nor absolute; it is Calliope who opens additional doors in the continuing search for truth, exemplified in this instance in the historical novels of German writers exiled after 1933.

Notes

Abbreviations

AdA	*Allemagne d'Aujourd'hui*
Afb	*Aufbau* (NY)
Akz	*Akzente*
AM	*Atlantic Monthly*
BA	*Books Abroad*
CC	*Christian Century*
CollG	*Colloquia Germanica*
Cw	*Commonweal*
DE	*Die deutsche Exilliteratur 1933–1945.* Ed. Manfred Durzak (Stuttgart: Reclam, 1973).
DEK	*Deutsche Exilliteratur seit 1933: Vol. I: Kalifornien.* Ed. John M. Spalek and Joseph Strelka (Berne: Francke, 1976).
DF	*Die Fähre*
DVLG	*Deutsche Vierteljahresschrift für Literaturwissenschaft und Geistesgeschichte*
EE	*Erfahrung Exil: Antifaschistische Romane 1933–1945: Analysen.* Ed. Sigrid Bock and Manfred Hahn (Berlin: Aufbau, 1979).
EuIE	*Exil und Innere Emigration.* Eds. Reinhold Grimm and Jost Hermand (Frankfurt/Main: Athenäum, 1972).
FH	*Frankfurter Hefte*
GJ	*Goethe-Jahrbuch*
GQ	*German Quarterly*

GR	Germanic Review
GRM	Germanisch-Romanische Monatsschrift (NS)
GuE	Geschichtsbewusstsein und Emigration. Der historische Roman der deutschen Antifaschisten 1933–1945. Elke Nyssen (Munich: Fink, 1974).
HB	Hermann Broch: Perspecktiven der Forschung. Ed. Manfred Durzak (Munich: Fink, 1972).
Hl	Helicon
IntL	Internationale Literatur
Kb	Kursbuch
LJ	Library Journal
LWuGP	Literaturwissenschaft und Geschichtsphilosophie: Festschrift für Wilhelm Emrich. Ed. Helmut Arntzen, Bernd Balzer, Karl Pestalozzi, and Rainer Wagner (Berlin: Walter de Gruyter, 1975).
MAL	Modern Austrian Literature
MG	Manchester Guardian
Mh	Monatshefte
MLQ	Modern Language Quarterly
MLR	Modern Language Review
MuW	Mass und Wert
NFT	Német Filológiai Tanulmányok
Nph	Neophilologus
NR	Neue Rundschau
NRp	New Republic
NSaN	New Statesman and Nation
NTB	Das Neue Tage-Buch
NY	New Yorker
NYHTB	New York Herald Tribune Books
NYTBR	New York Times Book Review
NZ	Die Neue Zeitung (Munich)
NZZ	Neue Züricher Zeitung
OL	Orbis Litterarum
PEGS	Publications of the English Goethe Society
PMLA	Publications of the Modern Language Association
Pt	Poetica
PT	Pariser Tageblatt
RhM	Rheinischer Merkur
RLC	Revue de Littérature Comparée
RLV	Revue des Langues Vivantes
SatRL	Saturday Review of Literature

SG	Studi Germanici
Sp	The Spectator
SZL	Das Silberboot: Zeitschrift für Literatur
TLS	The Times Literary Supplement
Trv	Trivium
UHR	Untersuchungen zum historischen Roman der deutschen Emigrantenliteratur nach 1933. Carl Steiner, Diss. George Washington University 1966.
WmS	Werkstattgespräche mit Schriftstellern. Horst Bienek (Munich: Hanser, 1962).
WuW	Welt und Wort
ZDP	Zeitschrift für deutsche Philologie
ZRdJ	Zeitkritische Romane des 20. Jahrhunderts. Ed. Hans Wagener (Stuttgart: Reclam, 1975).

1. Introduction

1. See E. M. Forster, *Aspects of the Novel* (New York: Harcourt, Brace & World, 1954), pp. 51–66.

2. Cf. Peter Härtling, *Das Ende der Geschichte: Über die Arbeit an einem historischen Roman* (Mainz: Akademie der Wissenschaft und der Literatur, 1968), p. 45.

3. Orville Prescott, *In My Opinion: An Inquiry into the Contemporary Novel* (Indianapolis: Bobbs-Merrill, 1942), pp. 134–36.

4. Hermann Kesten, *Der Geist der Unruhe: Literarische Streifzüge* (Cologne: Kiepenheuer & Witsch, 1959), pp. 31–32.

5. See Max Nussberger and Werner Kohlschmidt, "Historischer Roman," in *Reallexikon der deutschen Literaturgeschichte*, ed. Werner Kohlschmidt and Wolfgang Mohr, 2nd ed. (Berlin: Walter de Gruyter, 1958), I, 658.

6. "Der historische Roman. Versuch einer Übersicht," *Hl*, 3 (1940), 89–109.

7. See *Der Roman: Kleines Leserhandbuch*, 2nd enl. ed. (Freiburg i. Br.: Herder, 1954), pp. 65–81; and Golo Mann, "Geschichtsschreibung als Literatur," in *Deutsche Akademie für Sprache und Dichtung Darmstadt: Jahrbuch* (Heidelberg: Lambert Schneider, 1965), pp. 103–24.

8. *The Historical Novel*, tr. Hannah and Stanley Mitchell (New York: Humanities Press, 1965). See especially pp. 13–15, 23–29, 42–45, 53, 176–81, 192–95, 251. Lukács sees the essential aspects of his concept of the historical novel realized in the works of Scott. Cf. Forster, *Aspects*, pp. 51–66, for a radically different view of Scott.

9. Lukács, pp. 172–220.

10. Cf. Klaus Völker, "Brecht und Lukács. Analyse einer Meinungsverschiedenheit," *Kb*, No. 7 (Sept. 1966), 80–101.

11. *The House of Desdemona or The Laurels and Limitations of Historical Fiction*, tr. with foreword by Harold A. Basilius (Detroit: Wayne State University Press, 1963), pp. 11–16, 26, 72, 133–35, 138–44.

12. Alfred Döblin, "Der historische Roman und Wir," in *Aufsätze zur Literatur* (Olten: Walter, 1963), pp. 170–82.

13. Alfred Döblin, *Die literarische Situation* (Baden-Baden: P. Keppler, 1947), p. 29.

14. "Gestaltung und Lehre," *IntL*, 9, No. 6 (1939), 3.

15. Cf. Werner Mahrholz, *Deutsche Literatur der Gegenwart: Probleme, Ergebnisse, Gestalten*, ed. and rev. by Max Wieser (Berlin: Sieben-Stäbe, 1931), pp. 191–213.

16. R. Huch: *Von den Königen und der Krone* (1904), *Die Verteidigung Roms* (1906), *Der Kampf um Rom* (1908), *Das Leben des Grafen Federigo Confalonieri* (1910), *Wallenstein* (1915); J. Wassermann: *Caspar Hauser oder Die Trägheit des Herzens* (1908), *Das Gänsemännchen* (1915); A. Döblin: *Die drei Sprünge des Wang-lun* (1915); M. Brod: *Tycho Brahes Weg zu Gott* (1916); H. Mann: *Professor Unrat* (1905), *Der Untertan* (1918); E. Stucken: *Die weissen Götter* (1918); F. Werfel: *Verdi, Roman der Oper* (1924); L. Feuchtwanger: *Jud Süss* (1925); A. Neumann: *Der Teufel* (1926); I. Seidel: *Das Wunschkind* (1930).

17. E. G. Kolbenheyer: *Amor Dei* (1908), *Meister Joachim Pausewang* (1910), *Paracelsus-Trilogie* (1917–25); H. F. Blunck: *Werdendes Volk* (1925–28), *Die Urvätersaga* (1922–24); R. Hohlbaum: *Frühlingssturm* (1924–26); M. Jelusisch: *Hannibal* (1934), *Der Traum vom Reich* (1940).

18. Cf. Alfred Döblin, "Historie und kein Ende," *Die Zeitlupe: Kleine Prosa* (Olten: Walter, 1962), p. 194, and "Der historische Roman und Wir," p. 187.

19. Cf. Werner Vordtriede, "Vorläufige Gedanken zu einer Typologie der Exilliteratur," *Akz*, 15 (1968), 570–71; Ulrich Weisstein, "Bertolt Brecht. Die Lehren des Exils," in *DE*, pp. 380–81; and Manfred Durzak, "Laokoons Söhne. Zur Sprachproblematik im Exil," *Akz*, 21 (1974), 53–63.

20. Vordtriede, pp. 571–74. H. Mann, for example, never refers to his adversaries by name in his literary works, only in his polemical writings. Brecht similarly deleted the name Hitler from all of his poetry (573–74).

21. Joseph P. Strelka, "The Novel in German Exile Literature since 1933," lecture at the University of Kentucky in Lexington, 15 April 1971.

22. (Berlin: Dietz, 1966), pp. 114–49.

23. 2nd rev. and enl. ed. (Frankfurt/Main: Athenäum, 1968).

24. Diss. University of Southern California 1970.

25. (Munich: Beck, 1979).

26. Ed. Eike Middell, Alfred Dreifuss, Volker Frank, Wolfgang Gersch, Thea Kirfel-Lenk, and Jürgen Schebera (Leipzig: Reclam, 1979).

27. Ed. Reinhold Grimm and Jost Hermand (Frankfurt/Main: Athenäum, 1972), pp. 111–51; cf. Mahrholz, pp. 191–213.

28. (Stuttgart: Reclam, 1973).

29. (Berne: Francke, 1976).

30. (Stuttgart: Metzler, 1977).

31. (Berlin: Aufbau, 1979).

32. (Columbia, SC: Camden House, 1982).

33. Diss. Brown University 1964.

34. Diss. George Washington University 1966.

35. Diss. Leipzig 1971.

36. (Munich: Wilhelm Fink, 1974).

37. Renate Werner, "Transparente Kommentare. Überlegungen zu historischen Romanen deutscher Exilautoren," *Pt*, 9, Nos. 3–4 (1977), 324–51; Helmut Koopmann, " 'Geschichte ist die Sinngebung des Sinnlosen.' Zur Ästhetik des historischen Romans im Exil," paper delivered at the International Conference on German and Austrian Exile Literature, UCLA, 21–23 April 1983, to be published in the series, *Studien zur Literatur der Moderne* (Bonn: Bouvier).

38. *Die humanistische Front: Einführung in die deutsche Emigranten-Literatur*, Part I (Zurich: Europa, 1946), p. 82.

2. Analyses

1. Cordan's activities in the Dutch underground movement during World War II placed his life in constant danger. See Wolfgang Cordan, "Die notwendige Stille. Ein Wort von draussen," *SZL*, 3 (1947), 337–40.

2. Wolfgang Cordan, *Julian der Erleuchtete: Historischer Roman* (Zurich: Origo, 1950).

3. Although these are fictitious characters, Cordan assuredly intends reference to their historical counterparts. In the case of the Libyan, Euhemeros, the reference is to Euhemerus of Messene (ca. 340–260 B.C.), the Greek philosopher and mythographer who held that the gods of mythology were nothing more than deified mortals. The figure of Jamblichos refers to the grandson of Jamblichos of Chalcis (?–330), the definitive scholar of Neoplatonism who offered a systematic and methodical interpretation of Plato and connected the teachings of Plotin to mystical elements of the Orient.

4. This is one of the few passages which make direct reference to Cordan's contemporary world, for the problem of settling the Jewish people in a land of their own, following the persecution in fascist Germany, was of immediate concern. Other direct references can be seen in the theme of exile (13–16, 19–24) and the theme of political persecution which occurs throughout the novel.

5. Hans-Jürgen Seekamp, "Eros gegen Chaos. Wolfgang Cordans 'Julian der Erleuchtete,' " *NZ*, 22 July 1950, p. 11, cols. 4–5.

6. Cordan, "Nachwort," *Julian der Erleuchtete*, p. 549.

7. Ibid., p. 550.

8. Seekamp, p. 11.

9. *A Man Called Cervantes*, tr. H. T. Lowe-Porter (New York: Viking Press, 1935). First German edition: *Cervantes* (Amsterdam: Querido, 1934).

10. Cf. Virginia Chase Perkins, "Don Quixote's Creator," *Cw*, 21 (1935), 715; Ernst Toller, "Cervantes," *NSaN*, 8 (1934), 908; C. G. Poore, "A Living Portrait of Cervantes," *NYTBR*, 3 March 1935, p. 2; M. J. Benardete, "The Mask of Cervantes," *NRp*, 83 (1935), 110; and Ben Ray Redman, "Cervantes Brought to Life," *SatRL*, 11 (1935), 515.

11. *Cervantes: Ein Roman* (Stockholm: Bermann-Fischer, 1944).

12. In many instances, the facts surrounding vast portions of Cervantes' life are meager or nonexistent. The negative comments of Benardete in regard to

Frank's treatment of historical fact contrast sharply with those of Redman. Cf. Benardete, p. 110, and Redman, p. 515.

13. Toller, p. 908.

14. Ibid.

15. See especially Walter Carl-Alexander Hoyt, "Conflict in Change: A Study of the Prose-Fiction of Bruno Frank," Diss. Rutgers University 1978. Cf. Lion Feuchtwanger, "Zum Gedächtnis Bruno Franks," Afb, 11, No. 41 (12 October 1945), p. 18; and Virginia Sease, "Bruno Frank," DEK, pp. 352–70.

16. Steiner, UHR, p. 127.

17. Ibid., p. 132.

18. Cf. Harold von Hofe, "German Literature in Exile: Bruno Frank," GQ, 18 (1945), 88–89.

19. Steiner, p. 129.

20. The Queen's Doctor: Being the Strange Story of the Rise and Fall of Struensee, Dictator, Lover, and Doctor of Medicine, tr. Edwin and Willa Muir (New York: Alfred A. Knopf, 1936). First German edition: Struensee: Doktor, Diktator, Favorit und armer Sünder (Amsterdam: Querido, 1935).

21. Neumann's own utterances concerning this novel are negative, but his self-denigrating comments should not be taken altogether seriously, as the majority of his critics have done. Cf. Robert Neumann, "Unbekannt im Land— das mich entdeckte: Ein Selbstporträt," WuW, 16, No. 3 (1961), 77–78; Ein leichtes Leben: Bericht über mich selbst und Zeitgenossen (Vienna: Kurt Desch, 1963), p. 54; L. Cabot Hearn, "Dictator of Denmark," SatRL, 15, No. 7 (12 December 1936), 7; Louis MacNeice, "Fiction," Sp, 156 (29 May 1936), 994; Henry Steele Commager, "The Queen's Doctor," NYHTB, 6 December 1936, pp. 28, 37; J. D. Bereford, "Past and Present in New Novels," MG, 29 May 1936, p. 7; Harold Strauss, "Behind the Throne," NYTBR, 6 December 1936, p. 9; "Doctor-Dictator," TLS, 6 June 1936, p. 477; and Klaus Schröter, "Der historische Roman. Zur Kritik seiner spätbürgerlichen Erscheinung," in EulE, p. 132.

22. Cf. Carl Steiner, UHR, pp. 160–65. Steiner stresses only the fact that each book develops to a dramatic climax, a turning point in Struensee's career. He disregards the dynamics of the parallel forces which figure in each of the books.

23. Cf. Elisabeth Freundlich, "Die Welt Robert Neumanns," in Robert Neumann: Stimmen der Freunde: Der Romancier und sein Werk: Zum 60. Geburtstag am 22. Mai 1957 (Vienna: Kurt Desch, 1957), p. 76.

24. Cf. Freundlich, pp. 124–25. She discusses the abundance of outside sources employed by Neumann in his works.

25. Cf. Elke Nyssen, GuE, pp. 88–94. Nyssen erroneously uses the novel as an example for escapist literature of the German exile period.

26. Cf. Freundlich, pp. 75–76, 86–87. She stresses Neumann's practice of using the same building blocks to create different constructions in his novels. The stock market incident, for example, had been used previously in Sintflut.

27. Cf. Horst Bienek, WmS, p. 57. He stresses the point that literature was an expression of criticism of the contemporary world for Neumann, and as such, drew him into the political arena.

28. Cf. Steiner, p. 168. He quite rightly sees this as Neumann's presentation of the reverse side of the romantic idea of "Volksseele."

29. Cf. Steiner, p. 158. Steiner sees *Struensee* as a parody of the historical novel rather than a parody of politics in the form of a historical novel. It is, of course, both.

30. Cf. Bruce M. Broerman, "Robert Neumann's *Struensee*: Potboiler or Patent Parody?" *MAL*, 16, No. 2 (1983), 105–19. Broerman, in a more comprehensive study, refutes the majority of charges leveled against this novel.

31. *Don Pedro and the Devil. A Novel of Chivalry Declining*, tr. William Howard Wang (Indianapolis: Bobbs-Merrill, 1942). First German edition: *Don Pedro und der Teufel: Ein Roman aus der Zeit des untergehenden Rittertums* (Hamburg: Rowohlt, 1954).

32. The significance of making the novel a first person account is indicated to a certain extent in the quote by Sören Kierkegaard which precedes the first chapter, expressing that truth lies in subjectivity.

33. None of the critics of the day recognized the Parsifal theme and structure of the novel. Cf. Charles David Abbott, "Maass . . . ," *SatRL*, 15, No. 14 (4 April 1942), 13; Alice R. Eaton, "Don Pedro and the Devil," *LJ*, 67, No. 6 (15 March 1942), 268; Clifton Fadiman, "Various Conquerors, *NY*, 18, No. 6 (28 March 1942), 77–78; R. M. G., "Don Pedro and the Devil, *AM*, 169, No. 5 (May 1942), n.p.; W. E. Garrison, "An Empire Sickens unto Death," *CC*, 59, No. 18 (6 May 1942), 599; Milton Hindus, "Don Pedro and the Devil," *NYHTB*, 29 March 1942, p. 8; and Katherine Woods, "Don Pedro and the Devil," *NYTBR*, 29 March 1942, pp. 1, 30.

34. Maass' use of these contrastual elements does not indicate that he sees the figures and actions in the novel in terms of black and white. Such a simplistic portrayal would be inconsistent with the complex moral question which Maass is treating here, and none of his characters can be seen as entirely good or bad. Even the most damning portrayal of Pater Vicente cannot erase the fact that he acts with a certain degree of honest sincerity. Cf. Woods, p. 30.

35. Maass prefaces his novel with another quote, one taken from Walt Whitman's "Passage to India," which indicates that the present is nothing but an outgrowth of the past. Maass thus justifies the validity and logic of expressing the contemporary world through historical material.

36. Cf. Woods, pp. 1, 30. She was the only critic to recognize these parallels.

37. *The Pretender*, tr. Willa and Edwin Muir (New York: Viking, 1937). First German edition: *Der falsche Nero* (Amsterdam: Querido, 1936).

38. Steiner, *UHR*, pp. 34–36.

39. Cf. Andor Gabor, "Lion Feuchtwanger: 'Der falsche Nero,'" *IntL*, 7, No. 12 (1937), 136–37. Gabor mentions additional parallels not dealt with here.

40. Gabor, p. 136.

41. Nyssen, *GuE*, p. 148. Nyssen documents the literature pertinent to the relationship between Hitler and big business.

42. Gabor, p. 136.

43. This incident is described by Hans Leupold, *Lion Feuchtwanger* (Leipzig: VEB Bibliographisches Institut, 1967), pp. 50–51.

44. Cf. Marcel Reich-Ranicki, "Lion Feuchtwanger oder Der Weltruhm des Emigranten," *DE*, pp. 447–48; and Hermann Kesten, *Meine Freunde die Poeten* (Munich: Kindler, 1959), p. 171.

45. Cf. Alfred Antkowiak, *Begegnungen mit Literatur: Beiträge zur neuen*

deutschen Literaturkritik (Weimar: Thüringer Volksverlag, 1953), p. 228; and Gabor, p. 138.

46. Gabor, p. 138.

47. These are characteristic weaknesses which apply in varying degrees to many of Feuchtwanger's other historical novels. See Reich-Ranicki, pp. 444–54; and Hans Mayer, "Lion Feuchtwanger oder Die Folgen des Exils," *NR*, 76, No. 1 (1965), 120–29.

48. Cf. Lothar Kahn, "Lion Feuchtwanger," *DEK*, pp. 337–38. Kahn appears to agree with Feuchtwanger's defense of his position towards the Nazis.

49. Georg Lukács, *The Historical Novel*, pp. 338–39.

50. Cf. Werner Jahn, "The Meaning of 'Progress' in the Work of Lion Feuchtwanger," *Lion Feuchtwanger: The Man, his Ideas, his Work*, ed. John M. Spalek (Los Angeles: Hennessey and Ingalls, 1972), pp. 51–65.

51. Kesten, pp. 170–71. Kesten characterizes Feuchtwanger as being "thoroughly naïve and, in a naïve way, thorough." Later he calls him "very intelligent, but he believed he saw through the entire world, and he wanted to make it crystal clear to his readers, how the world really was and how thoroughly Lion Feuchtwanger saw through it."

52. Cf. Günther Heeg, *Die Wendung zur Geschichte. Die Konstitutionsprobleme antifaschistischer Literatur im Exil* (Stuttgart: Metzler, 1977), pp. 130–34; and Nyssen, p. 152.

53. *Young Henry of Navarre*, tr. Eric Sutton (New York: Knopf, 1937; *Henry, King of France*, tr. Eric Sutton (New York: Knopf, 1939). First German editions: *Die Jugend des Königs Henri Quatre* (Amsterdam: Querido, 1935); *Die Vollendung des Königs Henri Quatre* (Kiev: Staatsverlag der nationalen Minderheiten der USSR, 1938). For the sake of brevity, the complete work is referred to as *Henri Quatre*, Volumes I and II throughout.

54. Cf. Heinrich Mann, "Ein denkwürdiger Sommer," *IntL*, 6, No. 1 (1936), 22; "Gestaltung und Lehre," *IntL*, 9, No. 6 (1939), 3; *Ein Zeitalter wird besichtigt* (Berlin: Aufbau, 1947), p. 490; André Banuls, *Heinrich Mann* (Stuttgart: Kohlhammer, 1970), p. 169; Helmut Koopmann, "Der gute König und die böse Fee. Geschichte als Gegenwart in Heinrich Manns *Henri Quatre*," in *Untersuchungen zur Literatur als Geschichte*, ed. Vincent J. Günther, Helmut Koopmann, Peter Pütz, and Hans Joachim Schrimpf (Berlin: Erich Schmidt, 1973), pp. 522–44; Gerhard Köpf, *Humanität und Vernunft: Eine Studie zu Heinrich Manns "Henri Quatre"* (Berne: Lang, 1975), pp. 31–35; Ulrich Stadler, "Von der Exemplarursache zur Dialektik. Über den Gleichnischarakter von Heinrich Manns 'Henri Quatre,'" *LWuGP*, pp. 539–60; Manfred Hahn, "'Wahres Gleichnis.' Heinrich Mann: 'Die Jugend des Königs Henri Quatre' und 'Die Vollendung des Königs Henri Quatre,'" *EE*, pp. 169–92; and David Gross, *The Writer and Society: Heinrich Mann and Literary Politics in Germany, 1890–1940* (Atlantic Highlands, NJ: Humanities Press, 1980), pp. 256–60.

55. Cf. Eberhard Hilscher, *Poetische Weltbilder*, 2nd enl. ed. (Berlin: Der Morgen, 1979), pp. 44–45; Köpf, pp. 46–48; and Gross, pp. 259–62.

56. Cf. David Roberts, *Artistic Consciousness and Political Conscience: The Novels of Heinrich Mann 1900–1938* (Berne: Lang, 1971), p. 195; and Rolf N.

Linn, "Der Kontrast als Denk- und Sprachfigur in Heinrich Mann's *Henri Quatre*," *GRM*, 23, No. 2 (1973), 229–37.

57. Cf. Hanno König, *Heinrich Mann: Dichter und Moralist* (Tubingen: Max Niemeyer, 1972), pp. 303–14.

58. Cf. Roberts, pp. 211–15.

59. The following is a condensation of Roberts' presentation, pp. 196–210.

60. See Ulrich Weisstein, "Heinrich Mann, Montaigne, and *Henri Quatre*," *RLC*, 36, No. 1 (1962), 71–83.

61. Cf. Ulrich Weisstein, "Humanism and the Novel: An Introduction to Heinrich Mann's 'Henri Quatre,'" *Mh*, 51, No. 1 (1959), 18–19; *Heinrich Mann. Eine historisch-kritische Einführung in sein dichterisches Werk* (Tubingen: Max Niemeyer, 1962), p. 173; Georg Hünert, "Zu Heinich Manns *Henri Quatre*: Ein Bericht," *CollG*, 3 (1971), 301; Roberts, pp. 230–41; and Linn, pp. 233–35.

62. See Weisstein, *Heinrich Mann*, p. 173.

63. Cf. André Banuls, "Vom süssen Exil zur Arche Noah. Das Beispiel Heinrich Mann," *DE*, pp. 210–11.

64. Cf. Ernst Hinrichs, "Die Legende als Gleichnis. Zu Heinrich Manns Henri-Quatre-Romanen," *Text und Kritik Sonderband Heinrich Mann* (1971), pp. 111–12.

65. Cf. Gross, pp. 259–60; and Hahn, pp. 185–86.

66. Cf. Weisstein, "Humanism and the Novel," p. 16; and Gross, p. 258.

67. Letter to Félix Bertaux, dated 23 September 1934, quoted from *Heinrich Mann 1871–1950: Werk und Leben in Dokumenten und Bildern*, ed. Deutsche Akademie der Künste zu Berlin, intro. Alexander Abusch (Berlin: Aufbau, 1971), p. 256.

68. Cf. Roberts, pp. 162–89, 228–29; and Linn, pp. 232–33.

69. The trilogy first appeared as a two-volume work: *Die Fahrt ins Land ohne Tod* (Amsterdam: Querido, 1937) and *Der blaue Tiger* (Amsterdam: Querido, 1938). The availability of the entire trilogy in a single complete edition is so problematic that two partial editions were used. The third edition, *Amazonas* (Olten: Walter, 1963), was used for volumes I and II; the second volume of the first edition, *Der blaue Tiger* (1938), was used for volume III, references to which are indicated by the letters NJ (The New Jungle) before the page numbers. "Amazonas" is the title Döblin originally intended for the trilogy and has been used throughout. For more complete discussions of the problematics surrounding volume titles and text editions, see George Bernard Sperber, *Wegweiser im "Amazonas". Studien zur Rezeption, zu den Quellen und zur Textkritik der Südamerika-Trilogie Alfred Döblins* (Munich: Tuduv, 1975), pp. 8–9; Robert Minder, "Hommage à Alfred Döblin. Döblin en France," *AdA*, 3 (1957), 10; and Walter Muschg, "Nachwort des Herausgebers," *Amazonas*, p. 653.

70. See Döblin's own statements regarding the genesis of the trilogy in Alfred Döblin, *Aufsätze zur Literatur*, ed. Walter Muschg (Olten: Walter, 1963), pp. 393–94.

71. Cf. Döblin, *Aufsätze zur Literatur*, pp. 170–82; and *Die literarische Situation* (Baden-Baden: Keppler, 1947), p. 29.

72. Cf. Joseph Strelka, "Alfred Döblin. Kritischer Proteus in protäischer Zeit," ZRdJ, pp. 46–48; Jakob Erhardt, Alfred Döblins Amazonas-Trilogie (Meisenheim/Glan: Anton Hain, 1974), p. 3; Wolfgang Kort, Alfred Döblin: Das Bild des Menschen in seinen Romanen (Bonn: Bouvier, 1970), p. 107; and Muschg, p. 642.

73. See especially Alfred Döblin, Das Ich über der Natur (Berlin: Fischer, 1928); Unser Dasein, ed. Walter Muschg (Olten: Walter, 1964); and "Prometheus und das Primitive," MuW, 1, No. 3 (1938), 331–51. For a closer analysis of Döblin's views on nature, history, and religion, see Klaus Weissenberger, "Alfred Döblin im Exil. Eine Entwicklung vom historischen Relativismus zum religiösen Bekenntnis," CollG, 1/2 (1974), 37–51; and Adalbert Wichert, Alfred Döblins historisches Denken. Zur Poetik des modernen Geschichtsromans (Stuttgart: Metzler, 1978), pp. 75–84.

74. Kort, p. 113.

75. For opposing emphases, see F. Lion, MuW, 1 (1937–38), 141–45; and Erhardt, pp. 16–25.

76. Cf. Kort, pp. 107–8.

77. Cf. Erhardt, p. 23, who maintains that they are.

78. Cf. Wichert, pp. 192–97.

79. Ibid., pp. 148–51.

80. Cf. Kort, p. 116.

81. Ibid., p. 114.

82. Although Erhardt discusses many of the following points, he does not draw the connections between the actions.

83. Matthias Prangel, Alfred Döblin (Stuttgart: Metzler, 1973), pp. 82–83.

84. Cf. Kort, pp. 111–12; and Prangel, p. 83.

85. Cf. Manfred Auer, Das Exil vor der Vertreibung. Motivkontinuität und Quellenproblematik im späten Werk Alfred Döblins (Bonn: Bouvier, 1977), pp. 41–56; and Klaus Müller-Salget, Alfred Döblin, Werk und Entwicklung (Bonn: Bouvier, 1972), p. 379ff.

86. Today, most agree that Muschg's deletion of the third volume from his Amazonas edition and his justification for the deletion are indefensible. For further information regarding the criticism of this edition, see Roland Links, Alfred Döblin: Leben und Werk (Berlin: Volk und Wissen, 1965), p. 121; Hans-Albert Walter, "Alfred Döblin. Wege und Irrwege. Hinweise auf ein Werk und eine Edition," FH, 19 (1964), 871; Hansjörg Elshorst, "Mensch und Umwelt im Werk Alfred Döblins," Diss. Munich 1964, p. 102; Kort, p. 107; and Erhardt, p. 114.

87. The Ballad of the Hundred Days, tr. Moray Firth (New York: Viking, 1936). First German edition: Die hundert Tage (Amsterdam: Allert de Lange, 1935).

88. For conflicting views on the merits of this work, see Joseph Roth, Briefe 1911–1939, ed. and intro. Herman Kesten (Cologne: Kiepenheuer & Witsch, 1970), p. 412; Otto Forst de Battaglia, "Die Gabe des Berichtens: Joseph Roths Gesamtwerk," RhM, 1 March 1957, p. 8; and Garrett Mattingly, "A Glorious Illusion," SatRL, 14, No. 17 (22 August 1936), 5.

89. For a more comprehensive discussion of the novel, see Bruce M. Broer-

man, "Joseph Roth's *Die hundert Tage:* A New Perspective," *MAL,* 11, No. 2 (1978), 35–50.

90. Cf. Roth, *Briefe,* pp. 394–95; Alfred Döblin, "Joseph Roth: Die hundert Tage," *PT,* 1 December 1935, p. 3; Louis Kronenberger, "The Hundred Days," *NYTBR,* 30 August 1936, p. 7; Fritz Hackert, *Kulturpessimismus und Erzählform: Studien zu Joseph Roths Leben und Werk* (Berne: Lang, 1967), pp. 85–88; Hackert, "Joseph Roth: Zur Biographie," *DVLG,* 43, No. 1 (1969), 181; Helmut Famira-Parcsetich, *Die Erzählsituation in den Romanen Joseph Roths* (Berne: Lang, 1971), p. 106; Wolf R. Marchand, *Joseph Roth und völkisch-nationalistische Wertbegriffe: Untersuchungen zur politisch-weltanschaulichen Entwicklung Roths und ihrer Auswirkung auf sein Werk* (Bonn: Bouvier, 1974), pp. 310–14; Elke Nyssen, *GuE,* pp. 92–94; and David Bronsen, *Joseph Roth: Eine Biographie* (Cologne: Kiepenheuer & Witsch, 1974), pp. 565–66.

91. See Frank Trommler, *Roman und Wirklichkeit: Eine Ortsbestimmung am Beispiel von Musil, Broch, Roth, Doderer und Gütersloh* (Stuttgart: Kohlhammer, 1966), p. 63; Bronsen, *Joseph Roth,* pp. 71–184, especially pp. 102–23; and Bronsen, "The Jew in Search of a Fatherland: The Relationship of Joseph Roth to the Habsburg Monarchy," *GR,* 54, No. 2 (1979), 54–61.

92. Trommler, p. 63.

93. Carl Steiner, *UhR,* p. 226.

94. Cf. Famira-Parcsetich, p. 107.

95. Cf. Hackert, "Joseph Roth: Zur Biographie," p. 181; Famira-Parcsetich, p. 108; and Marchand, pp. 301–2.

96. Cf. Marchand, p. 303.

97. Steiner, p. 221.

98. This is not recognized by many critics. Cf. Steiner, p. 228; Nyssen, pp. 88, 92–94; Bronsen, *Joseph Roth,* pp. 565–66, 571–72; Famira-Parcsetich, pp. 106–08; Marchand, pp. 303–14; Döblin, p. 3; Leo Parth (=Hermann Wendel), "Die hundert Tage," *NTB,* 14 December 1935, pp. 1194–95; Alfred Kazin, "Forlorn Little Man Back From Elba," *NYHTB,* 23 August 1936, p. 7; Kronenberger, p. 7; and Mattingly, p. 5.

99. Cf. Nyssen, p. 92; Steiner, p. 221; and Werner Sieg, *Zwischen Anarchismus und Fiktion. Eine Untersuchung zum Werk von Joseph Roth* (Bonn: Bouvier, 1974), pp. 74–77.

100. Cf. Hackert, *Kulturpessimismus und Erzählform,* p. 88; and Mattingly, p. 5.

101. Cf. Hackert, "Joseph Roth. Zur Biographie," p. 181; Marchand, p. 311; and Sieg, pp. 71–74.

102. Cf. Marchand, p. 313.

103. *The Beloved Returns. Lotte in Weimar,* tr. H. T. Lowe-Porter (New York: Alfred A. Knopf, 1940). First German edition: *Lotte in Weimar* (Stockholm: Bermann-Fischer, 1939).

104. Cf. Bernhard Blume, *Thomas Mann und Goethe* (Berne: Francke, 1949), pp. 93–95; and Charlotte B. Evans, "Das Goethebild in Thomas Manns 'Lotte in Weimar,'" *Mh,* 63, No. 2 (1971), 105–16. Blume documents the meager facts surrounding the historical encounter between Charlotte and Goethe; Evans

charges Mann with destroying Goethe's original identity, overlooking the fact
that preserving that elusive identity was not Mann's intent.

105. Cf. Barbara Molinelli-Stein, "Grösse als Gewissensfrage," *GJ*, 98 (1981),
207–13. She posits her interpretation of Goethe's Color-Tetraeder, rather than
the Werther experience, as the formal structural principle.

106. Cf. Uve Fischer, "Die Begegnung Mann-Goethe im VII. Kapitel von *Lotte
in Weimar*. Anmerkungen zum Parodiebegriff bei Thomas Mann," *SG*, 13
(1975), 389–98. Fischer is only one of many who place such emphasis on
chapter seven.

107. Cf. János Barta, "Vision oder Wirklichkeit? (Über die Schlussszene der
Lotte in Weimar)," *NFT*, 9 (1975), 17–26. Barta offers interesting, and in many
respects correct, observations about the nature of the final chapter, but is
unable to integrate these convincingly into the structure of the novel.

108. Cf. Hermann Kunisch, "Thomas Manns Goethe-Bild," in *Thomas Mann
1875–1975. Vorträge in München-Zürich-Lübeck*, ed. Beatrix Bludau, Eckhard
Heftrich, and Helmut Koopmann (Frankfurt/Main: Fischer, 1977), pp. 327–29.
Kunisch emphasizes the ironic character of the entire work.

109. E. Havenith, "Bemerkungen zur Struktur des Goetheromans 'Lotte in
Weimar,'" *RLV*, 27, No. 4 (1961), 330.

110. Cf. Molinelli-Stein, p. 222.

111. Cf. Agnes E. Meyer, "A New Novel by Thomas Mann. 'The Beloved
Returns' Is a Book With a Message for Our Time," *NYTBR*, 25 August 1940,
p. 21.

112. Cf. Erich Heller, *The Ironic German: A Study of Thomas Mann* (London:
Secker & Warburg, 1958), p. 29; Inge Diersen, *Untersuchungen zu Thomas
Mann: Die Bedeutung der Künstlerdarstellung für die Entwicklung des Realis-
mus in seinem erzählerischen Werk* (Berlin: Rütten & Loening, 1965),
pp. 193–95; Eberhard Hilscher, *Thomas Mann: Leben und Werk* (Berlin: Volk
und Wissen, 1966), pp. 103–9; Meyer, p. 21; Olaf Ludmann, "Einige Gedanken
zum Thema 'Goethe als literarische Gestalt'," *GJ*, 97 (1980), 132–33; Herbert
Lehnert, "Repräsentation und Zweifel. Thomas Manns Exilwerke und der
deutsche Kulturbürger," in *DE*, pp. 401–8; Hinrich Siefkin, "*Lotte in Weimar*—
'Contactnahme' and Thomas Mann's novel about Goethe," *Trv*, 13 (1976),
38–52; and Fischer, pp. 389–98.

113. Cf. Hinrich Siefkin, "The Goethe Centenary of 1932 and Thomas
Mann's *Lotte in Weimar*," *PEGS*, 49 (1978–79), 84–101.

114. Cf. William V. Glebe, "The 'diseased' artist achieves a new 'health'.
Thomas Mann's *Lotte in Weimar*," *MLQ*, 22 (1961); and Diersen, p. 196.

115. Cf. Eike Middell, "Ein Goetheroman, ein Deutschlandroman. Thomas
Mann: '*Lotte in Weimar*,'" in *EE*, pp. 193–220; and Diersen, pp. 196–97.

116. Cf. Georg Lukács, *Essays on Thomas Mann*, tr. Stanley Mitchell (London:
Merlin Press, 1964), pp. 40–41.

117. Cf. Siefkin, "The Goethe Centenary of 1932," p. 92; and Heinz Lüdecke,
"Thomas Manns dialektisches Goethe-Bild," *Afb*, 8 (1952), 941.

118. Gerhard Lange, *Struktur- und Quellenuntersuchungen zur "Lotte in
Weimar"* (Bayreuth: Tasso, 1970). Lange presents a thorough study of the
sources Mann used and how they were transformed in the novel.

119. Cf. Molinelli-Stein, p. 193, who points out the parallel to Goethe's own literal use of a report by Kestner on Jerusalem for *Werther*.

120. Cf. Keith Dickson, "The Technique of a 'Musikalischideeller Beziehungskomplex' in 'Lotte in Weimar,'" *MLR*, 59 (1964), 421–23. Dickson deals with this aspect in greater detail.

121. Cf. Ludmann, pp. 136–39.

122. Cf. Hilscher, p. 115.

123. Cf. Diersen, p. 207; and Thomas Mann's letter to Kerényi of 18 February 1941 in Thomas Mann, *Gesammelte Werke*, 12 vols. (Berlin: Fischer, 1955), 2: 757.

124. Cf. Hilscher, p. 115.

125. Cf. Gustav E. Mueller, "On Thomas Mann's 'Lotte in Weimar,'" *BA*, 19 (1945), 236. Mueller criticizes the novel on exactly this basis, claiming it is weakened.

126. Meyer, p. 1.

127. *The Death of Vergil*, tr. Jean Starr Untermeyer (New York: Pantheon, 1945). First German edition: *Der Tod des Virgil* (New York: Pantheon, 1945).

128. See Theodore Ziolkowski, "Broch's Image of Vergil and Its Context," *MAL*, 13, No. 4 (1980), 6–18, who discusses Broch's image versus Broch's knowledge of these facts.

129. Because of the specific context in which Broch's novel is treated in this study, no attempt is made to provide a comprehensive analysis of Broch's synthesis of art, aesthetics, ethics, theory, philosophy, time, politics, history, morality, and social consciousness. For in-depth discussions of these elements in isolation or combination see Hermann Broch, "Geschichtsmystik und künstlerisches Symbol," *DF*, 1, No. 1 (1946), 41–47; Aniela Jaffé, "Hermann Broch: 'Der Tod des Vergil.' Ein Beitrag zum Problem der Individuation," in *HB*, pp. 135–76; Erich Kahler, *Die Philosophie von Hermann Broch* (Tubingen: Mohr, 1962); "Werttheorie und Erkenntnistheorie bei Hermann Broch," in *HB*, pp. 353–70; Dietrich Meinert, *Die Darstellung der Dimensionen menschlicher Existenz in Brochs "Tod des Vergil"* (Berne: Francke, 1962); John J. White, "Broch, Virgil, and the Cycle of History," *GR*, 41, No. 2 (1966), 103–10; Timm Collmann, *Zeit und Geschichte in Hermann Brochs Roman "Der Tod des Vergil"* (Bonn: Bouvier, 1967); Louis F. Helbig, "Hermann Brochs Roman Der Tod des Vergil als Dichtung des Gerichtes über die Dichtung," *MAL*, 2, No. 1 (1969), 7–20; Ernestine Schlant, "Hermann Broch's Theory of Symbols Exemplified in a Scene from Der Tod des Vergil," *Nph*, 54, No. 1 (1970), 53–64; *Die Philosophie Hermann Brochs* (Berne: Francke, 1971); "Zur Ästhetik von Hermann Broch," in *HB*, pp. 371–84; Hermann Krapoth, *Dichtung und Philosophie. Eine Studie zum Werk Hermann Brochs* (Bonn: Bouvier, 1971); Robert A. Kann, "Hermann Broch und die Geschichtsphilosophie," in *HB*, pp. 385–98; Joseph Strelka, "Hermann Broch als Exil-Autor," *MAL*, 8, No. 3/4 (1975), 100–12; Malcolm R. Simpson, *The Novels of Hermann Broch* (Berne: Lang, 1977), pp. 77–96; Børge Kristiansen, "Hermann Broch's Roman 'Der Tod des Vergil,'" *OL*, 32, No. 2 (1977), 116–39; Endre Kiss, "Zur Theorie und Praxis des modernen Romans—Über Hermann Brochs 'Der Tod des Vergil,'" *Nph*, 62, No. 2 (1978), 279–89; Karl Menges, "Bemerkungen zum Problem der ästhetischen

Zeitgenossenschaft in Hermann Brochs *Der Tod des Vergil*," *MAL*, 13, No. 4 (1980), 31–49; and Maria Angela Winkel, *Denkerische und dichterische Erkenntnis als Einheit. Eine Untersuchung zur Symbolik in Hermann Brochs Tod des Vergil* (Frankfurt/Main: Lang, 1980).

130. Cf. Hermann J. Weigand, "Broch's Death of Vergil: Program Notes," *PMLA*, 62 (1947), 531–47. The following discussion of these climaxes follows, to a certain extent, the presentation of Weigand.

131. For further reading see Joseph P. Strelka, *Kafka, Musil, Broch und die Entwicklung des modernen Romans* (Vienna: Forum, 1959); Walter Hinderer, "Die 'Todeserkenntnis' in Hermann Brochs 'Tod des Vergil,'" Diss. München 1961; and James N. Hardin, "The Theme of Salvation in the Novels of Hermann Broch," *PMLA*, 85, No. 2 (1970), 219–27.

132. Hermann Broch, *Dichten und Erkennen* (Zurich: Rhein-Verlag, 1955), p. 268. See also Götz Wienold, "Die Organisation eines Romans. Hermann Brochs 'Der Tod des Vergil,'" *ZDP*, 86, No. 4 (1967), 571–93.

133. Broch, *Dichten und Erkennen*, p. 266.

134. For a more comprehensive discussion of Broch's style in all its aspects, see Klaus Heydemann, *Die Stilebenen in Hermann Brochs "Der Tod des Vergil"* (Vienna: Notring, 1972); Fritz Martini, "Hermann Broch. Der Tod des Vergil," in *Das Wagnis der Sprache: Interpretationen deutscher Prosa von Nietzsche bis Benn* (Stuttgart: E. Klett, 1954), pp. 408–64; Wieslawa Erna Wolfram, "Der Stil Hermann Brochs. Eine Untersuchung zum 'Tod des Vergil,'" Diss. Freiberg i. Br., 1958; and Arno Köhne, "Stilzerfall und Problematik des Ich. Stilkritische Studie zur Sprache von Hermann Brochs Roman 'Der Tod des Vergil,'" Diss. Bonn, 1961.

135. The following paraphrases Walter Hinderer, "Grundzüge des 'Tod des Vergil,'" in *HB*, pp. 108–9.

136. Broch, *Dichten und Erkennen*, pp. 266–67.

137. See Ziolkowski, pp. 18–22.

138. Hermann Broch, *Briefe*, ed. Robert Pick (Zurich: Rhein-Verlag, 1957), p. 244.

139. Broch, *Dichten und Erkennen*, p. 265.

140. All examples cited from Manfred Durzak, "Zeitgeschichte im historischen Modell. Hermann Brochs Exilroman 'Der Tod des Vergil,'" *DE*, p. 435.

141. Broch, *Briefe*, p. 244.

142. Cf. Wilhelm Grenzmann, *Dichtung und Glaube: Probleme und Gestalten der deutschen Gegenwartsliteratur* (Frankfurt/Main: Bonn: Athenäum, 1966), p. 138.

143. Cf. Broch, *Briefe*, p. 403. For a broader background, see Hermann Broch, *Gedanken zur Politik* (Frankfurt/Main: Suhrkamp, 1970), especially the section "Verteidigung der Demokratie," pp. 37–131.

144. Hermann Broch, *Erkennen und Handeln*, ed. Hannah Arendt (Zurich: Rhein, 1955), p. 321.

145. Strelka, "Hermann Broch als Exil-Autor," pp. 106–10.

3. Conclusion

1. Cf. Nussberger and Kohlschmidt, I, p. 658.
2. Cf. Wehrli, pp. 89–109.
3. Cf. Abusch, *Literatur im Zeitlater des Sozialismus; Lukács, Skizze einer Geschichte der neueren deutschen Literatur;* Jarmatz, *Literatur im Exil;* Schröter, "Der historische Roman"; Dahlke, "Geschichtsroman und Literaturkritik im Exil"; and Nyssen, *Geschichtsbewusstsein und Emigration.*
4. Cf. Mahrholz, pp. 191–92.
5. Cf. Henri R. Paucker, "Exil und Existentialismus. Schwierigkeiten einer Wiederbegegnung," *NZZ,* 15/16 November 1975, p. 62.
6. Cf. Döblin, *Die literarische Situation,* p. 29.

Indexes

Names

Subjects